Sliding

Sliding

A Journey through Post-Traumatic Stress Disorder After a Fatal Car Crash

Connie Jo Bachman
written with Kimberly Younkin

iUniverse, Inc.
New York Bloomington Shanghai

Sliding
A Journey through Post-Traumatic Stress Disorder
After a Fatal Car Crash

iUniverse books may be ordered through booksellers or by contacting:

iUniverse
1663 Liberty Drive
Bloomington, IN 47403
www.iuniverse.com
1-800-Authors (1-800-288-4677)

Because of the dynamic nature of the Internet, any Web addresses or links contained in this book may have changed since publication and may no longer be valid.

The views expressed in this work are solely those of the author and do not necessarily reflect the views of the publisher, and the publisher hereby disclaims any responsibility for them.

ISBN: 978-0-595-38974-2 (pbk)
ISBN: 978-0-595-83356-6 (ebk)

Printed in the United States of America

*I would like to dedicate this book
to the life and memory of
Patricia Marie Sloan*

Author Note:
Reading this Book

In this book, I tell the story of my struggle with surviving a fatal car accident and healing from resulting post-traumatic stress disorder. My hope is that my story illustrates the symptoms of the disorder and its companion condition, survivor guilt, and gives you resources to help you in your healing.

Although I am not a psychologist, I did have input from my own clinical psychologist in writing this book and did extensive research on PTSD. To assist you in understanding and identifying the disorder and its stages, I have inserted 'Self-Help" notes after certain chapters where I felt my research would be useful to you. You can read them at the end of the chapters, or continue with the story and return to the notes as you choose.

There is also a Resource List at Appendix "A" that includes organizations and support groups. The book's Bibliography lists wonderful books written by medical professionals and experts in trauma victim care. I hope you will find these useful in your recovery.

Contents

Part III—Hope

Acknowledgments

To my amazing therapist, my savior and my inspiration for writing this book. I was so incredibly blessed to have found you and I thank you for everything from the bottom of my heart.

To Kim Younkin, for believing in my story and in my telling of it. Your talents are exceptional and it was such a pleasure to work with you. Thank you for your support, patience and dedication.

To my Mom and my family. I love you all very much.

And to my many friends.

Introduction

The day you get your driver's license, it's cause for celebration. You never, ever think that someday, with no warning, you'll be behind the wheel—and hit someone and kill them.

But it happens. To people who haven't been drinking. To everyday people, and celebrities—like first lady Laura Bush, actors Matthew Broderick and Rebecca Gayheart, singer Brandy, and former Miss America Heather French.

And it happened to me. On a crisp, bright morning in December 1977—an ordinary day—I left home a sixteen year-old girl with everything to live for. And I ended up being involved in an accident that tragically killed another person. In one moment, my life and the lives of others were irrevocably changed. Yes, it was an accident. But it's with me every day of my life.

In this book, *Sliding: A Journey through Post-Traumatic Stress Disorder after a Fatal Car Crash,* I chronicle my experience as the survivor of a fatal automobile collision—an experience shared **but rarely discussed** by thousands of Americans each year—and my resultant struggle with and treatment for post-traumatic stress disorder.

Categorically defined in 1980 by the American Psychiatric Association as an anxiety disorder after the Vietnam War, post-traumatic stress disorder affects millions of individuals surviving child abuse, suicide, natural disasters and other traumas. Although the disorder is widely researched, with over 200 how-to-cope and treatment books in print today and support networks including The National Center for Post-Traumatic Stress Disorder (PTSD) and the PTSD Alliance, the population of motor vehicle accident survivors with PTSD is under-studied.

Today, the single leading cause of PTSD in the general population is motor vehicle accidents. Each year there are over 6 million police reported accidents in the United States with over 2.6 million injuries and 42,000 deaths. An average of 117 people die every day in motor vehicle crashes—one every 12 minutes. In the past 10 years, nearly 420,000 fatalities occurred, making motor vehicle accidents the leading cause of death for persons of every age from 3 through 33 years old. It is estimated that 9 percent of survivors of serious accidents develop significant post-traumatic stress symptoms and that many other survivors have PTSD-like reactions.

Despite these staggering numbers, most of the six existing publications on PTSD in motor vehicle accident survivors are clinical or statistical in nature and address only assessment and subsequent treatment. The remaining few, though emotional self-help guides, contain few testimonials to which other similar sufferers can relate. There are no books in print wholly devoted to the true, uncensored story of a motor vehicle accident survivor's struggle with PTSD.

Sliding: A Journey through Post-Traumatic Stress Disorder after a Fatal Car Crash is the **only book written *by* a survivor of a fatal car accident and PTSD *for* similar survivors.** The book details my disorder's progression and its associated "survivor guilt" to help others identify their own symptoms. My story will include notes from my treating clinical psychologist and also key notes from skilled professionals as it relates to trauma and survivor guilt. It is my hope that my story will provide a kinship to those suffering in silence and urge them to reach out for help to begin their own healing process.

Unresolved trauma-related feelings never go away. They always live inside you, swept up in a neat little pile of dust until something comes along and kicks it and makes a mess of them again.

Part I—Trauma

Chapter 1

On a crisp, bright morning in December 1977, I left home a sixteen year-old girl with a full, carefree teenager's day ahead of me. I returned hours later, my life and the lives of others forever altered by an event I could not have imagined and had difficulty believing even after it happened.

The day was chilly and brisk but snow had not yet fallen in the Midwest. I walked out the door of my family's farmhouse in Sunbury, Ohio, and met brilliant sunshine and a rush of cold air against my face. I closed my eyes and smiled as I opened the door of the car parked outside.

I was a junior and basketball player at Big Walnut High School, off to another day in my young world. Each was more or less the same. I drove myself the twelve miles to school, picking up nearby friends on the few days I did not have practice after classes. Then it was home for dinner with my mother and older brothers and homework and time to think more about basketball.

On the weekends, we played games. Afterward, I worked on the farm, spent time with my school friends, and went to church with my family on Sunday before my weekly routine repeated itself.

It was my life. Some of us are blessed with the gift of excelling at something, or even many things—an art form, a skilled craft, a professional discipline, a sport, an intellectual pursuit. My thing was basketball. My coaches paid me a high compliment when they invited me to play on the varsity team the year before, and there I remained. I played more than one position and did not really care which, as long as I was in the game, surrounded by my closest friends.

That morning, my team was on my mind. We had been preparing diligently for an upcoming game, a fierce rivalry we looked forward to with the Utica Redskins. That day after school would be our last practice before meeting our foes on the court the following night. As I maneuvered the green Dodge Polara out of the driveway and onto the road for the long drive to school, the magnificent day and thoughts of my team winning made me beam.

I popped an eight-track tape into the car's player, and sang along with the Pure Prairie League's "Amie" as I drove, tapping my fingers on the steering wheel. It was a teenager's morning, untroubled and innocent.

All changed in an instant.

*   *   *

Two miles from my house, I stopped at the intersection at State Route 605, the two-lane country road that led into town. I turned right, straightened the car, accelerated.

As the car gained speed, it slid on a patch of black ice.

I lost all control. The car drifted around the slippery road like a novice skater unable to find sure footing. Neither my frantic turns of the wheel nor my foot on the brake would keep it from crossing the centerline.

The oncoming car appeared just then as if taking a cue to enter the stage. We crashed head-on in a deafening explosion, two cannons tearing into metal.

The impact was massive and soul-jarring and quick. It threw me forward into the steering wheel, my face smashing against its center column. Our mangled cars stopped abruptly in the ditches on opposite, wrong sides of the road.

Then there was silence, a quiet as thick as if the sky had dropped its first and deepest snow of the season on top of us, all at once.

*   *   *

For long moments I sat, stunned and bleeding. My limbs would not move. I felt heavy, as if someone was sitting on me. Shock prevented me from detecting pain; I could not sense whether anything was broken, whether my extremities were still attached. I was aware of blood falling onto my shirt, but could not feel the wound or lift my hand to find it.

I could not say how long I sat there. It was long enough for someone to have seen or heard the crash because I remember a man appearing from nowhere to sweep the littered glass from the road. He worked intently, his head bowed and eyes focused on the head of his broom, as if the pieces were a shameful stain he could not bear to leave in place. The man did not approach either car to check on the condition of their drivers. I watched from my car as he swept and swept, clearing the road of debris.

Finally, I raised my right hand and turned the rearview mirror to see my reflection. I saw my upper lip torn from its place—completely detached from my mouth and rammed into my cheek. Blood poured from the wound and my broken nose, but I had little reaction to the sight. The thought it conjured was that the accident may be serious, that the other driver may also be injured, perhaps severely.

The other car's front end had collided with the front passenger side of mine; it had propelled me around in a half circle so that, when my car reached a stop, it was backed into a ditch facing the intersection I had just left. I looked away from the mirror and back to the road to see a third car approaching from the direction I had come. As it neared, I watched it slide on the same black ice. It headed directly toward me as it spun out of control. I felt no fear, made no attempt to cover my face with my arms; I simply waited for it to hit me. But no impact came. It slid past me and stopped.

With great care, I opened my door and attempted to step out. I had not yet seen any movement from the other car and no one—other than the man with the broom and the third car—had arrived at the scene. I swung my left leg out, feeling it imperative that I get to the other car to check on its driver, but I lost my balance as I tried to stand and fell into the ditch. As I lay there, I saw two people emerge from the third car; it was my friend, Tina, and her brother, Kevin, the friends I would have driven to school on a day without basketball practice. I would ask myself countless times in my life what would have happened if there had been no practice scheduled that day, if ten more minutes had passed while I picked them up.

Tina ran to me and helped me to my feet.

"Oh my God, Connie, are you alright?" she asked with a worried look. Without waiting for an answer, she said, "Here, let's sit back in the car."

"No, I...," I began, trying to tell her I needed to get to the other car. I remained standing, but swayed.

She held my arm to steady me.

"You're okay," she said softly.

Other cars had begun to stop and people were gathering around the scene. Some were helping the sweeping man clear glass and debris from the road, and a small crowd had gathered around the other car. I tried to walk in that direction but my legs crumbled again. Tina was there.

I looked at her and said, "Please find out about the other driver for me."

"Others are taking care of it," she assured me as I leaned on her. "Come on, now, let's get you back in the car. Someone will be here real soon to help."

I stood and stared at the other side of the road before allowing Tina and some other passersby to lead me back to my car (Kevin had left immediately to inform my mother). Tina held her hand behind my head as I leaned back into the seat. She covered me with a coat since I had not worn my own, to calm my shivering and comfort me.

I huddled there, wondering if anyone had called for help, waiting for an ambulance to arrive. I thought of the other driver, the extent of injuries. I had not seen anyone emerge from the car.

I asked someone who was hovering around my car, "Did someone call an ambulance?" Yes, he was certain one had been summoned.

I waited.

Time seemed eternal from the moment of the crash; what was probably only moments to an onlooker was a long day and the start of another for me. I could not understand why help was taking so long to arrive. Maybe the medics did respond quickly, but my mind's injury prevented me from thinking lucid thoughts.

Where are they? What is taking the other person so long to get out of the car?

The words tumbled around in my head, fast and then faster in my growing panic

Through the windshield I saw my brother, Rick, a volunteer firefighter called to the scene with no idea I was involved in the accident, running toward me.

"Connie!" he cried. "Are you okay?"

"Yes," I replied. "Rick, please, will you check on the other driver?"

"In a minute," he said, crouching next to me and taking my head in his hands through the open car door. "Let me look at you first."

Gingerly, he turned my face from side to side, surveying my injuries. After a few moments, in which I again pleaded for him to go see, he nodded and said, "I'll be right back. Okay?" Then he walked toward the other car and I watched him sink into the mass of people across the road.

I screamed inside. *Where is the ambulance?!*

More long minutes, seemingly longer than real time, passed before I heard sirens. *Finally.* But I was briefly relieved. The sounds soon faded as the medics turned in the wrong direction and headed away from the scene.

No! Where are they going? We're over here!

I was screaming inside and felt no movement of time. I sat rooted to the driver's seat, straining to hear the sirens again and willing help to come.

Finally, the ambulance found its way and stopped in front of us and one paramedic ran to me, one to the other car. He covered my mouth to control the bleeding and examined me for additional injuries. All the while I looked toward the other side of the road, waiting.

I watched as the crowd that had gathered around the other car turned slowly and seemed to walk directly toward me. *Something is wrong. What is it? What's wrong?* Rick appeared by my side and helped me onto a stretcher. I saw him turn his head to speak to the paramedic about where they would take me, but his voice was distant, his face blurred. My mind and body seemed to disappear.

The other driver never got out of the car.

<u>Self-Help Note: Understanding Trauma</u>

Trauma—what is it?

The American Heritage® Dictionary of the English Language: Fourth Edition (2000) defines "trauma" as "a serious injury or shock to the body, as from violence or an accident"; "an emotional wound or shock that creates substantial, lasting damage to the psychological development of a person, often leading to neurosis"; and "an event or situation that causes great distress and disruption."

Trauma and its effects can arise from car accidents, sexual and physical abuse, natural disasters like floods, fires and hurricanes, plane crashes, terrorist attacks, violence in schools, wars, and other catastrophic and overwhelming events. The wound can be physical or emotional, or both.

At the onset of the trauma, most people experience symptoms of shock, even if they're mild. The length of the shock stage varies depending upon the person and the traumatic event they have experienced. Here are some of the ways shock manifests itself:

- Disorientation and confusion, a "dazed" or "numb" feeling
- Lack of pain with a physical injury
- Emotional detachment (in my case, when I had little reaction to the sight of my injured lip or the fact that a car was sliding toward me on the ice)
- Disbelief in the occurrence of the event
- Immediate (and lasting) disturbance of the memory of the event
- Physiological reactions such as loss of blood pressure and disturbance of vital body functions

Some shock symptoms may remain even when the initial shock stage dissipates.

Chapter 2

As I lay staring at the ceiling of the ambulance on the way to the hospital, I knew. No one took my hand and told me that the other driver had died in the crash; it was unnecessary. A soft blanket of denial swaddled me, a buffer keeping out the sounds of the paramedics' voices and the click-beep, click-beep of the medical equipment that spat out my vital signs.

I scarcely noticed when the ambulance skidded out of control on the icy roads. Somewhere outside me a voice exclaimed, "Oh, no!" The driver struggled to regain a hold on the vehicle; another said, more calmly, "Looks like the roads are still pretty slick." Still I stared at the fixed point above me. I did not speak, or ask questions, or beg for my mother. I lay there entranced by the white metal roof as if God Himself had adorned it. The stupor, of course, was my brain's way of blocking the horrible truth that a person who had been living an hour before was gone.

My mother was the only person who spoke the words.

She had been on the heels of the ambulance since Tina had hastily dispatched Kevin to collect her. It must have been dreadful listening to screaming sirens and wondering how badly I was injured.

But my mother had been through hardship. Vera Jean Bachman—Jean, to all who know her—married my father at a young age and accompanied him through his dream of becoming a farmer. They milked cows, harvested crops, raised cattle. She bore five children, three to start. After that, they planned to wait some years to have three more. But when they got to me, the fifth, my father was diagnosed with Hodgkin's disease. My mother nursed him through his illness until he died at the young age of 43. I was eight, and my mother had me, my brother, the family farming business and my older siblings to care for and manage. She did it all with strength and grace and dignity.

She found me waiting for her in a room in the emergency area. Ever composed, she did not react to the bloody bandages across my face.

Leaning over and kissing me on the forehead, she asked, "How are you, honey?"

My answer was barely audible. "I'm okay."

I asked, as well as I could through my injury and the dressings, "How is the other driver?" and prayed my instincts would be wrong.

She sat down and took my hand, squeezing it tightly. She looked away, searching for words, then back at me.

"She didn't make it."

I did not respond. My hand went limp in hers, then my whole arm. Inside, I seemed to implode, the news a detonation that reduced my heart to ash.

My mother's words were still hanging in the air when two police officers entered the room and pressed me for a statement. They stood in front of the bed in their starched uniforms with expressionless faces, pens drawn, and conducted their business professionally and quickly.

I hated them.

They had to get my statement now, they said. It could not wait until I felt better or could speak coherently. "How fast were you driving before the crash?", and "Were you driving the speed limit?", and "Are you sure about your speed?" were some of the seemingly fifty ways they asked me if the accident was my fault. I answered furiously and uncertainly, more to get them to put away their obscenely inappropriate notepads than to provide information.

"I really don't know how fast."

They asked one last time, forcefully, "How fast do you *think* you were going?"

I didn't know. I thought back to where I was when we hit, and guessed.

"I don't know. Maybe fifty miles per hour."

They left and I was transferred to another hospital where, later that day, an oral surgeon performed the first of many operations to repair my mouth. The doctors anesthetized me for the outpatient procedure since they had to reattach my upper lip to my gum. I felt nothing. Afterward they covered my face in fresh bandages. The bandages were to aid in healing, of course—to help new skin grow and fuse with the old. But to me the dressing was a refuge. Behind it, I hid not only my wounds, but also the guilt and shame that took root that day.

I returned home in the late afternoon. The familiar walls of my house seemed less vivid—colors muted, pictures unfocused, light suspended hazily in the air. I felt numb, and hollow, as if I would shatter like thin glass dropped on tile.

I thought of my team at practice, where I fervently wished I could be, dribbling the ball with only the lingering of a horrible nightmare. That I had been involved in another person's death was not within my comprehension, so my mind kept busy trying to will backward the hands of the clock.

*   *   *

Our phone rang constantly for the next few days and the house was full with friends and family. My immediate family alone was rather large; though most of my siblings had left home, they all were in the house for those few days, hovering, entertaining guests, waiting on me. Linda was twenty-nine and married with two children of her own. Chuck was twenty-seven and Rick, twenty-six. My parents' "second family" had ended up being only me, and my brother, Wayne, four years my senior.

The mood was subdued and people spoke in hushed voices as they came and went. Always upbeat, my family did not know what to say, or how to comfort me.

Sadness was something they just did not do.

I sat and received the guests, my mind weaving like a drunkard. Fog enveloped me for long periods. Then, it would lift and I would see things more clearly, focus on a face that was looking at me and hear their words. It would last only briefly, until I smiled at a comment or heard laughter from the kitchen. Then, reality struck me with a near-physical blow; I would remember someone was dead, and the fog would return.

In the midst of my family and well-wishers I felt utterly alone. I sat on an uncharted island of feeling. No one had been where I was or felt my desolation.

No one said what I needed to hear.

What do you say when someone you know and love has been in a crash in which another person died? Do you broach it and risk saying something insensitive though well intentioned? What if you try to be heartfelt and wise, but your words are too upsetting? And what if the year is 1977, when people didn't talk about family or individual problems or crises—let alone death—and dealt with trauma by burying it far inside in the hope it might disappear?

You say "I'm thinking of you," or "I'm praying for you," or "I hope you make a quick recovery." Meaning well, that's what everyone said. Each one pushed me further into withdrawal from myself and my former teenage life.

*   *   *

A few days later, as I sat quietly with my friend, Jeanette, my mother told me that she and my father's parents were going to the funeral home.

"Do you want to come with us, Connie? You can if you want to. But you don't have to, you know. People will understand."

She was going to pay her respects to Patricia Sloan—Pat, to her family and friends; the twenty-nine year-old married mother of two small children who had been driving the other car. I had survived the crash and she had not, and now there would be a funeral. A minister or priest or rabbi would stand in front of a coffin that held her body and talk to the congregation about her life and death and then they would put her in the ground and put a stone on the earth above her. Everyone there would witness that she would never again walk or talk or play with her kids or love her husband.

Did I want to go?

Oh my God, what do I do?

Pat's death was impossible to believe. I had not known her or spoken to her, or ever seen her face. But she had been just like me—human, living her life on a weekday. She had been just like my sister, Linda; they were the same age, both mothers of two. She had been just like all of us living in a small country town making a long trek from home to work or school because nothing was close to home in peaceful country life. As she drove, she might also have been listening to a favorite song, similarly buoyed by the beautiful day.

She could have been me, and I her.

If I went, my injuries would make it obvious I was the other driver. My young mind created visions of Pat's family attacking me, verbally and physically; I pictured angry people staring and pointing.

"There she is—she killed Pat!"

"You should be in jail! My daughter is dead because of you!"

I imagined these and equally ugly words, people cursing me. I knew I could not survive such torment. Overwhelmed by destructive thoughts and colossal guilt at even being alive to make the decision, I chose not to attend.

"No, Mom. I don't think I can go," I said. It took every bit of will I had not to break in half in front of Jeanette, sitting next to me with her head bowed, and my mother, walking out the door to do a most difficult deed. I held it together.

It was not until my friend left that I went to my room, closed the door, and sobbed. I thought of my mother, standing in the congregation on my behalf, the mother in the crowd who still had her daughter. I struggled with whether my decision to stay away was the right one. I waited for my mother to return.

When she did, I was there.

I inhaled deeply. "What happened, Mom?"

She looked tired. "I spoke with Mr. Sloan, her husband," she replied. "He was very nice to me, and I could tell he appreciated that we came."

I wanted to know more, whether Pat's children were there, how they seemed to be holding up, what words were said about Pat. I wanted to know every detail. But my emotions were too close to the surface, and my mother had been through enough for one day. So I kept my questions to myself.

*   *   *

The winter holidays came just a week after the accident. Though it was a blessing to be away from school and whispers in the hallways, I mostly thought of two young children opening their gifts on Christmas morning without their mother, and a young husband trying to keep it together for his kids without collapsing. A few times, I found myself enjoying a holiday moment, but then reality quickly rushed in and I felt fresh waves of guilt for celebrating. What right did I have to take pleasure in the day when so many others grieved a death that involved me?

When I was not thinking of the people who loved Pat Sloan, I was thinking of the people at school—my friends, teachers, kids in my classes I did not know. I knew they all would be talking about me, curious about my involvement in the crash. In fact, I later discovered that before I returned to school, rumors had circulated that I had died in the accident. I dreaded going back there, hearing it, but the few weeks at home were brief. Soon, I had to stop envisioning my return and face it.

When the day came, I still had a narrow strip of bandage across the top of my upper lip and into my cheeks, and as I walked the halls for the first time since the crash, I felt as if the seas had parted to let me pass. Eyes bored into me—with questions, with pity, and it seemed to me, with accusations.

I almost heard the words in the minds of those who walked past me.

That's her, the girl from the bad accident.

Poor girl, she looks terrible.

I wonder if it was her fault.

Their thoughts buzzed in my head, a white noise that hummed incessantly and dulled my senses. Even the support of my close friends could not diminish the feeling that I was alone. The whole world could have held me in a warm embrace that day and year and I still would have felt vacant inside.

Self-Help Note: Reactions to Trauma

"Each person reacts to trauma in a unique fashion, depending on the partic-
ulars of the trauma and the person's unique self and history. Your emotional
makeup, personal, family and relationship history, age at the time of the
trauma, social and cultural relationships, previous coping strategies, avail-
ability of support before, during and following the traumatic experience—all
these factors shape the meaning of the event for you. [ ] Traumatic events
shake the foundation of a person's life."

- excerpted from *Life After Trauma* by Dena Rosenbloom, PhD and Mary
  Beth Williams, PhD

Even if two people experience the same traumatic event, they may process it
differently in that one may consider it a "bad experience" and the other, a
trauma that affects their entire lives. Regardless, both people may experience one or many of the common physical, mental, emotional and behav-
ioral reactions to trauma, including, but not limited to: nausea, dizziness,
nightmares, difficulty making decisions, changes in the way you think about
the world, other people and yourself, detachment from others and disconnection with yourself, guilt, anger, depression, sadness, fear, and inability to
enjoy life. (For a more exhaustive list, see *Life After Trauma*, p.19, Table 1.1:
"Some Common Reactions to Trauma.")

It's easy to chalk up these reactions as attributable to something else, like
stress at work or in interpersonal relationships-especially if they're still
occurring months or years after the traumatic event. But these signs could be
indicative of a serious condition, that, left untreated, could have lifelong
ramifications. You should seek the attention of a knowledgeable professional
as soon as you notice the occurrence and continuance of these reactions.

Chapter 3

The last half of my junior year was distinctly different from the first.

I went from an above-average student with perfect attendance to a struggling, unfocused student who fell asleep in class and received detentions as punishment. I missed days of school for doctor appointments and subsequent cosmetic surgeries on my lip.

The crash did not leave me disfigured, but I had a hard time seeing myself when I looked in the mirror. I had my senior photographs taken three times for the yearbook, since in the first two sets my injury seemed to scream at me from the page. I didn't want to look back at it and see Connie Jo Bachman, Accident Survivor. I was sixteen years old and wanted to look normal.

Returning to the basketball court gave me some relief. The doctors did not restrict me from play and I resumed practices and games just after the holiday break. On the court, I was the "old" Connie. My teammates passed no judgment on me and I looked forward to the sanctuary they gave me from what I saw as others' prying eyes. I only missed a few days of practice because of follow-up medical care.

I also missed school and practice for meetings with lawyers.

*   *   *

The legal meetings were to prepare my defense for a trial on the charge of vehicular homicide. Since I had crossed the centerline in the crash, the county prosecutor would try to prove negligence. The crime was a first-degree misdemeanor and if found guilty, I would face a fine, a license suspension, imprisonment of up to six months, or a combination of penalties.

I had never been in trouble and it stretched the limits of my comprehension that I would be a defendant on trial for a death. Fear consumed me, but it was not *for* me. I had overheard a conversation at home between my mother and a brother as we prepared for trial.

They had been talking in hushed voices in the kitchen as I stood around the corner, listening.

"Didn't the lawyer say something about restitution?" I heard my brother whisper. "What if we have to pay?"

My mother's muted voice replied, "Yes, I know."

"There's nothing except the farm."

My mother was calm. "I know."

She never mentioned this conversation to me—in fact, my mother said nothing about the charge or the trial outside our lawyer's office. Horror seized me when I heard those words—the thought that my family might lose the farm we worked so hard to maintain after my father died was unbearable.

The farm was our family's sole source of income. We were one of the larger farming families in our small community; we produced milk for the Lawson's chain of convenience marts, harvested nearly four hundred acres of corn and beans annually, and raised large herds of beef cattle. It was, since my father and mother had moved from the city, our existence.

was terrified that my family's reputation and lives would be destroyed; that we would lose everything and I would be to blame. I begged God not to let that happen, pleaded with Him to relieve my pain and the pain I had caused others. I prayed for strength to relive the accident during the trial, and that Pat's family would not be in court as I did. I was scared I would fall apart if they were there.

But the Sloans did not attend the pretrial conference or the trial, and I was relieved to bear the events without their scrutiny.

The issue in court was whether I was driving too fast on the wintry roads and, if so, whether excessive speed caused the accident. I sat at the defendant's table for half a day and listened to the prosecutor do his best to make me feel worse than I did (a formidable task). He used my emergency room statements to the police to prove his case. The crash had occurred near the end of a thirty-five mile-per-hour zone; I had told the police I was going fifty. By my own statement, it looked like I had been speeding.

My mother sat next to me and we listened to the legal arguments. We sat in silence, making no contact and looking straight ahead at the judge, and heard our lawyer recount the facts of the accident.

"On the morning of December sixteenth, Connie Jo Bachman left her house for the twelve-mile drive to Big Walnut High School. She stopped her car approximately two miles from her home at a stop sign on Center Village Road, and then turned right onto State Route 605." He paused. "As she was accelerating out of the thirty-five mile-per-hour zone on 605, her car's tires slid on a patch of black ice. The icy conditions were not visible to Connie. She lost control of the car and could not regain it, despite her efforts. She slid into the path of Patricia Sloan's car, which was traveling out of a fifty-five mile-per hour zone. Their cars collided."

He paused again and looked intently at the judge.

"Those are the facts, Your Honor. Connie Bachman was not negligent. She was a victim of circumstance."

My lawyer called Tina and Kevin to testify on my behalf. They had arrived at the scene after the crash, but they told the judge I was a reliable person, a careful driver and a friend—things that were true and helpful. They said things I could not say on my own behalf; my lawyer helped me decide that I would not testify because I could barely keep my emotions in check.

After closing arguments and my lawyer's last urging that there had been no wrongdoing on my part, the judge acquitted me of the charge.

The verdict brought some relief and, in my mind, saved my family from further humiliation and possible destitution. The moment the judge issued his verdict, I wanted out of that courtroom. I wanted to throw open the doors and run as far as the next county. I wanted to be with my friends and forget about everything if just briefly, by sitting on the bench at that evening's game and pretending I was the Connie of the past November, the starting point guard, the team motivator calling plays and giving mid-court pep talks.

My mother drove me straight to the game from the courthouse, and I walked quickly to the locker room where my teammates huddled for a halftime game recap. I opened the door and they sat there as if waiting for me.

Choking sobs lodged in my throat, stifling words. Instead, I smiled and gave my friend, Peggy, who had already started to walk toward me, a thumbs-up sign that said, "Everything's okay." She reached me and quickly wrapped her arms around me. Then the whole team followed and surrounded me, their arms offering comfort and love.

*   *   *

With the events connected to the accident over—Pat's funeral, my trial, my reconstructive surgeries—it seemed logical that I would begin to heal. There was nothing to do *but* heal at that point. My face healed. The broken nose mended itself and the traces of surgical knife marks on my lip faded as the days passed. I did not play a part in my physical healing; it happened on its own with the help of learned professionals, the miraculous power of the human body and the grace of God.

Unfortunately, there was no alliance of man, self and the Divine to heal me on the inside, no village to come together on my behalf to relieve the swelling of the ugly internal bruises.

Not one teacher at my school approached me, from the accident until the day I received my diploma and a handshake, to ask me how I felt. No school counselor, staff member or any person in an administrative role said a word to me about the crash or asked how I was coping with Pat's death in the eighteen months I remained associated with them.

Today, schools bring in teams of counselors and therapists to deal with student trauma—school shootings, teenage suicide and drug abuse, family and student deaths. It's the age of mental health awareness. School counselors probably make weekly classroom visits to discuss problems relevant to the age group and to plug their services. That is as it should be.

But it was 1977. Nearly thirty years ago. No one even discussed mental health assistance and counseling then, let alone utilize either. Then, school counselors existed only to administer tests and prepare students for college admission, not counsel teenage kids through massive trauma. People in general didn't know what to do or how to help.

So, at least in my case, they completely ignored it. It was as if people believed grief would go away if left alone.

That ignorance made my mind my worst enemy.

My family, loving though it was, was in shock. They had no idea how to handle such a horrific event so they also chose to avoid it. No one spoke of the accident in my house after Pat's funeral. Ever.

It was surreal, the reaction of those around me, as if the crash was a hiccup in my life and would eventually go away.

As a result, I had no guidance in processing my painful thoughts and feelings. No one reached out to help; I took that as an implicit instruction not to ask for it. I began to slowly self-destruct, constantly berating and criticizing myself.

Enormous amounts of grief and guilt and shame consumed me. They were a cloud over me each day, so dark someone should have noticed it. Pat was gone, and fate's decision was final. Someone older with more knowledge and life experience may have been able to tell me why, or at least helped me make sense of the world's random chaos.

But there was no one.

As a result, shame and guilt began to work their magic. When, years later, came across the article "Healing from Shame Associated with Traumatic Events" by Dr. Angie Panos, I recognized my sixteen year-old self in her words:

> Shame is a deep, debilitating emotion, with complex roots. Its cousin are guilt, humiliation, demoralization, degradation and remorse. After experiencing a traumatic event, whether recent or in the distant past shame can haunt victims in a powerful and often unrecognized manner Shame impairs the healing and recovery process causing victims of trauma to stay frozen, unable to forgive themselves for being in th wrong place at the wrong time. Shame leaves victims with feelings of sadness and pain at the core of their being. They are unable to feel th fullness of joy in their lives. *** Shame can dissolve positive self-esteem

and leave victims of trauma feeling different and less worthy and in some case bad or evil themselves. The trauma and the resulting shame potentiate each other, causing greater intensity in the psychological wounds. The end result is that the traumatized person no longer feels worthy of being loved, accepted, and having good things happen to them in their life.

Indeed, as I learned through intensive therapy twenty-five years later, my negative and harmful feelings began to grow, unchecked, from that year forward.

They eventually formed my new belief system about the world and my role in it: the world does not make me feel safe, and I do not deserve to be happy.

Self-Help Note: The Importance of Supportive Relationships

It cannot be emphasized enough the importance of supportive relationships with caregiving others after you or someone close to you has experienced a traumatic event. The existence of a support network is crucial for healing—especially since, after the event, it is common to feel isolated, as if "no one can understand."

If you have experienced trauma personally, reach out to your supportive others. **Ask for help.** If you *are* a supportive other, it is imperative that you show your willingness to help the victim of the trauma—*even if you feel that any actual help you could give would be insignificant.*

> "When someone you love has difficulties, listen. When you're feeling terrible that you can't provide a cure, listen. When you don't know what to offer the people you care about, listen, listen, listen."
> —Bernie Siegel, M.D.

It's not uncommon to feel as if the relationships you have with your support network are challenged after you experience a trauma. Even those who love you may not know how to help you. They may not understand what you're going through, and feel confused, afraid and helpless—and you may feel more of a loss because of it. They may not be used to seeing you struggle, and they may struggle themselves with wanting to take away your pain, yet not knowing how.

But there are many places to look for support, in addition to caring family members and friends. They can include coworkers, church members, school guidance counselor, or your family doctor. Also, your local newspaper is a great resource for area support groups, which can be especially helpful for someone who does not feel comfortable sharing their feelings with someone they know.

Chapter 4

Every day after the crash, I thought of the Sloan family in places where I should have thought about nothing at all—while watching television, folding laundry, setting the table for dinner, taking out the trash, and looking for the mate to a shoe. Sadness, and disbelief at life's abrupt change, were my constant companions. Deep sorrow smothered my heart and I desperately wished I could share it with Pat's family. I wanted to tell them I was sorry, that I *did* care (I convinced myself that, because I didn't go to the funeral home, they would forever think I didn't). I wanted them to know I was devastated. But I didn't know how.

When you're sixteen you look for someone to say it's okay to send flowers and write a letter, or at least find you an address and cry with you while you write. You hope someone will ask if you're strong enough to phone them, or if you need help making the call. You want someone to lead you through your grief, or at least let you lie on their lap and cry until your tears dry up—even though you're a big girl now.

That "someone" not to be, I grieved underground. I relied on coping mechanisms of my own design. They were ill-conceived and detrimental to my well-being; they were glaring, exploding-firework signs that I was not well.

I withdrew, fixated, and began to drink.

The only social things I engaged in for the rest of high school were basketball and occasional outings with friends. But I was not nearly as social as before. None of my friends had been through a similar experience or understood where I was; when I was with them I turned off their chattering and sat in silence.

Pat had been the wife of Michael, and the mother of seven-year-old Timothy and five-year-old Bonnie. She had also been a daughter, a sister, a niece and an aunt.

I became consumed with wondering how her family was coping with her death, especially her children.

Every day I thought of a little boy and girl, living not far from me in a house filled with grief, struggling to adjust to life without their mother. I was acutely aware of what lay ahead for them. There were things they would never do with their mother and things they would never experience with her gone, as I learned when my father died. Their mother would not heap their plates with steaming mashed potatoes and gravy at dinner before sitting to begin a prayer. She would not scream herself hoarse in the stands as they raced around with their team on a sporting field, or marched across it carrying a tuba. There would be no birthday parties given by mom, with the sweet warm aura about it only she can give. She would not snap hundreds of pictures of them as they left for their proms and their graduations and put straight pins in the stray hems of their gowns and robes and trousers as they left the house. There would be no mother of the bride or groom at their weddings.

The maternal light in their lives had been extinguished. And it would be worse for Bonnie, because a young daughter growing up without her mother is the cruelest of fates.

I thought of them as I went through teenage motions. When the school bell rang and I walked silently to my next class, I wondered if they knew about me, whether they hated me. As I pulled on my clothes and shoes for practice, I imagined two small, unsmiling faces, cheeks wet with tears. When I sat at dinner with my own mother and looked at my father's empty seat, I thought of the open seat at the Sloans' table. And in the evenings, when I told my mother I was going to a friend's house and instead drove around alone for hours, I wished I could drive backward through time and bring those children's mother back.

Sorrow never left me. I wanted so badly to express it to Pat's family and her little children, but could not imagine how. The only thing I could think to do was visit Pat's grave. So, that's what I did, again and again and again.

The day of my first visit, I drove to the nearby Village of Centerburg, Ohio, where Pat's family lived, and stopped at a gas station to ask for directions to the cemetery. There were two. I drove to the first and walked through it, stone by stone, reading hundreds of names of the dead, but did not find her grave. After another long search at the second, I did. I stopped and stood in front of her headstone, shaking.

It said "Mother," and her name, and the dates of her birth and death. I read it just once, then dropped to my knees and sobbed.

I didn't stay long that first time; terrified that someone, especially one of Pat's family, would find me and want revenge for her death, I quickly left the cemetery. I visited her grave alone for many months, and would continue to, telling no one, as the years passed.

My desire to know about the family became an obsession. One day on my way to the cemetery, I stopped at a phone booth and looked up their address. Then I drove by their house, a farm with fenced-in acres of grazing horses and a swing dangling from a towering tree in the front yard, in hopes of seeing children playing there, maybe even smiling—any sign to tell me they were coping as well as they could. I wanted some assurance that life would go on for them and they might have a chance at happiness.

I didn't see any children that day or any other. In my many visits to the cemetery and trips past the Sloan house in the first years after the crash, I never encountered another person.

The visits and drive-bys were how I coped with what I could never change; all the while wishing I could change it.

And I drank.

I drank to drown my self-pity—the "why did this happen to me?" and "aren't I supposed to be having the time of my life?" questions. I drank because I lived and Pat did not, and because I did not have any say in the matter. I did it to escape reality. It was something my family never knew, and if they knew, they never mentioned it. I just wanted to slightly dull my senses. It was so much more comfortable there, in that blurry place. My mind didn't work as well; I could shut up for just a little while.

On a few evenings, I told my mother I was going out with friends just so I could get away and be alone. I drove and thought and cried, then came home and snuck into bed.

One evening, I found myself at a park. I sat in the dark, replaying the accident over in my mind and wondering how my life had come to this point. Emotion quickly overwhelmed me. The tears came hard and fast and I sobbed uncontrollably as I had done from time to time since the accident. After a long while, I reined in my emotions and left. I was not on the road long before I looked in the rearview mirror and saw the person behind the wheel—a little girl with red, swollen eyes; exhausted, and in no way fit to be driving a car.

My friend lived close to the park, so I pulled into her driveway to rest before driving home. I was so tired. I wanted to go to sleep and never wake up. I thought, as I had thought many times since Pat's death, *If I could just die, everything would be okay again.* I wished death would come for me, too, to make up for the death I felt I had caused.

I had just closed my eyes and laid my head back on the seat when my friend, Sheri, tapped on the car window, her face clouded with worry.

"Connie, what are you doing?" she asked fearfully. "Are you okay?"

I rolled down the window and started crying again.

I watched her look me over and saw it register with her that I should not be driving. She hesitated only a moment and then said, "I'm going inside to wake my parents. I think we need to call your mom. Just wait here."

I didn't resist.

I sat in the car, crying, for the few moments it took for my mother to arrive. When she pulled into Sheri's driveway, Sheri and her parents were waiting with me near my car.

My mother remained in her car as I hung my head and walked around to the passenger side. She looked out at Sheri's parents and said, "Thank you for the call," before driving us away.

The ride home was quiet, with only my feeble attempts to brush off the evening breaking the silence.

"I'm so sorry, Mom," I said, looking out the window of the passenger seat as she drove. "I don't know what I was thinking."

I didn't tell her why I had done it, or that the crash might as well have killed me too.

*   *   *

My slow descent continued through high school. In my mind, I did not deserve to live any life, especially not a happy one. Why was I living when someone else was dead? How could I allow myself happiness when the accident had destroyed so many lives? How could I go on as if nothing had happened?

Self-help Note: Self-Blame and Survivor Guilt

How many of us have thought, when something awful has happened, *What if I had done X? What if I hadn't done Y? Would this still have happened?*

Even when a traumatic event takes place outside our control, we're human beings, and human beings sometimes blame themselves for the occurrence. When this happens, we go over and over the event in our minds, telling ourselves that the car accident would not have happened if we'd only taken a different route, that we would not have been physically or sexually abused if we had been a "good" boy or girl or wife or child.

Many people who survive a trauma where another person dies or is injured or severely mistreated believe that they could have prevented that harm to the other person. They spend inordinate amounts of time imagining "if-then" situations that may have changed the outcome, regardless of the lack of logic and wealth of emotional defense mechanisms in that thinking. It is normal to feel such feelings; we're only human. In fact, it's healthy to feel some form of survivor guilt in that it affirms that you are a caring, empathetic individual. *But you must seek help if you feel it become overwhelming or, as in some cases, obsessive.*

"The devastating event that occurred to you is important in itself. Also important, however, are your attitudes toward that event. Whether you have survived one trauma or several, your beliefs about why the trauma occurred and the way you judge your behavior during and after the traumatic episode are going to heavily influence the degree to which you continue to suffer."

- excerpted from *I Can't Get Over It: A Handbook for Trauma Survivors* by Aphrodite Matsakis, Ph.D.

As Dr. Matsakis also states in *I Can't Get Over It*, "people prefer to think that they are able to control their lives, so it is easier to blame themselves for negative events than to acknowledge that sometimes life is unfair or arbitrary and innocent people can be victimized for no reason."

Part II—Disorder

Chapter 5

I finished high school in 1979, seventeen months after the crash. After that, I ran.

Columbus, Ohio was thirty minutes from home. The state capital and a busy city, it seemed a good destination. I took a job at the Columbus Airport as a sales representative for the Hertz rental car company as soon as I got my diploma. The commute gave me time to think, usually about the Sloan family. I still thought of them and the crash every day and drove by their house occasionally. My visits to the cemetery continued, but I always kept them brief for fear of discovery.

The change gave my mind a constructive focus. It helped some.

It took little time to meet new people. Mary Ann Jacob also worked at Hertz that summer, and we quickly grew close. When I started college that fall at Columbus Technical Institute to pursue an associate's degree in business, I packed my belongings and moved from my mother's house into an apartment in Columbus with my new friend. My relief at leaving Sunbury was considerable. I would never again have to drive the route that had led to Pat's death, or walk the streets of the small town wondering what people thought of me as they passed. I knew I would return for nothing more than a family visit.

I made other friends, joined the college women's basketball team. New surroundings and anonymity were blessings—no one knew about my past, and I did not tell them. In that way, I made sure my new friends would not determine my guilt or innocence or think less of me for what had happened. It was easier to keep others at a distance, to peel back only my superficial layers.

My friendship with Mary Ann was different from the others. From the start, it seemed as if we had always known each other and our bond quickly became solid. It has been for years.

She spread happiness with her perky demeanor, contagious laugh and bright sense of humor. When we were together, I felt like the "old" me I lost in the crash—my mood was always upbeat and I felt eighteen instead of eighty. It was easy to be with Mary Ann and to confide in her.

One day, without having planned it, I told her about the crash.

I remember the immense relief at finally sharing my past with someone who cared about me, and in hearing her compassionate and concerned response.

Mary Ann remembers the moment this way:

> We were sitting on Connie's bed in our apartment playing backgammon, cross-legged with the board between us, chatting. She mentioned it nonchalantly, slipping it into the conversation without much emotion. I was terribly sad that she had experienced something so painful at such a young age, but her lack of emotion made me assume she was handling it well. She told me about the song she had been listening to when their cars crashed, and afterward, I watched her react to it whenever we heard it on the radio. Connie never reacted dramatically or showed any emotion when she heard it, though now I know what must have been going through her mind each time.

In telling Mary Ann what weighed on my mind and heart every day, I finally felt a lifeline to another human being instead of one adrift. She had listened, hurt with me and cared about me. To at least *one* person, my past was not shameful In the disclosure (that's what I considered it, as if I were a criminal disclosing a violent past) I gained a safety net; *at least Mary Ann is there*, I would think.

Life moved on and I tried to move with it, albeit in an emotionally disabled way. tried to focus on each day as a college student athlete with studies, classes, test and games. I forced myself to be fully in the present. At the same time, guilt and shame still weighed heavily on my heart as it had done for nearly two years. later learned that it was that time in my life when I began to slowly, subcon sciously lock away the torment.

Three years after we became roommates, Mary Ann and I gained another. Patt Steward moved in with us in 1983 and soon became another close and truste friend. I eventually told her about the crash, too, but, as with Mary Ann, th telling was more factual than emotional and I did it without forethought. I jus wanted her to know, I didn't think to ask for help with it.

*   *   *

Years passed. Instead of navigating my emotional wreckage, I worked and socialized with friends and traveled. The crash was always in my mind but lingered at the periphery. I still cried for Pat and her family and for me, but the tears were less frequent, and the complete breakdowns—"spells", as I sometimes called them, where sadness erupted and I cried for hours to get some relief—were fewer and farther between.

What did not change, as I turned twenty-five, and twenty-seven, and thirty, was my longing to know that Pat's family had survived their loss. I wanted to picture them—especially her children, Tim and Bonnie—adjusting to a new life and even being happy sometimes, but I had no proof and it haunted me. At times during those years, I was so desperate to know about them that I considered hiring a private investigator. I kept track of how old the children were each year. Pat's son Tim—*Is he driving yet? Did he get married? Has he had children?* I would wonder. He was her older child, only nine years my junior. Bonnie was two years younger than Tim, five when her mother died. When I thought of her growing from a girl into a young woman without her mother to guide her, I could almost feel my heart's seams rip.

*   *   *

Over those fifteen years, I lived life in this way. On the outside, I looked like a normal woman. I graduated from college and started one business, then another. After several years of entrepreneurship, an opportunity arose in corporate logistics. I took a job as a dispatcher and gradually moved up the proverbial ladder. I dated, but did not marry. I bought houses. I did things grown-ups do.

I did all this behind a façade, telling few people who I really was and what was in my heart. I was two people—the woman wearing the mask and the one behind it.

I have lived over half of my life in secret.

It was never an option to discuss the crash and my feelings about it with any member of my family. Despite a close relationship with my mother and good relationships with my siblings, we did not speak of it. The accident had been painful for them, too. My mother had attended the funeral home on all our behalves, and stood by me during the trial. Although she never mentioned it, I'm sure there were other things she endured but spared me knowing. It was difficult for all of them, and I believe they were as supportive as they knew how to be. Over time, it seemed better that my feelings remain unspoken.

Other than Mary Ann and Patty, I only spoke of the crash to those with whom I became emotionally involved. Even then, the telling was an item on a checklist like a full disclosure prerequisite. I didn't want to hide it and risk losing someone I cared about in the future because I wasn't honest from the start.

I hated every second of the revelation. I wanted to be honest, but I always expected the other person to become distant and think less of me, as if I had committed some heinous, purposeful crime. I always watched their eyes, looking for evidence of disgust, revulsion and blame. It never came. In a decade of dating, no one ever ran after hearing my story.

The odd thing was, despite this, I still expected it each time I met someone new.

Even though my secret never scared anyone away, the few relationships I had in those years did not last—and it was usually because I ended them. I later learned through therapy that I probably ended them because of the guilt I felt over Pat's death. Looking back, I can hear my damaged mind's questions as I became close to someone.

Why would anyone love you, Connie? How can you allow yourself this happiness when you caused someone's death?

Instead of opening up as I became close to someone, I shut down and eventually walked away.

In *Trust After Trauma*, Dr. Aphrodite Matsakis explains how guilt can manifest itself in the interpersonal relationships of trauma survivors:

> Building an emotional wall around yourself is another consequence of trauma-related guilt. You fear becoming close to others because if you are truly comfortable and relaxed around another person, one day you may talk about aspects of the trauma about which you feel guilt and shame. Then that person may reject or leave you. You don't trust that you can have a close relationship and not, inadvertently, mention something about the trauma that will frighten or disgust the other person.

As a result, you wall out other people, or are very guarded about how close you let anyone come to you.

I didn't understand at the time how much the guilt had penetrated my belief system. I felt responsible, and, in turn, worthless, inadequate and completely undeserving of love. Even nearly fifteen years after the accident, I had not forgiven myself and could not expect that forgiveness in the form of acceptance and love from another.

*   *   *

When I met Jamie, I was in my thirties and I thought I had put the worst of the accident's aftermath behind me. My private emotional collapses had become infrequent. I had managed to bury the pain, but there was always the waking and looking in the bathroom mirror and *knowing.* I knew that would always be there but I had learned to live with it and thought I had everything under control.

Jamie and I were friends for some time before we realized there was something special between us that seemed to go beyond friendship. We began dating and it soon came time for the crash revelation. I dreaded baring my past again, opening the Pandora's Box of internal guilt and shame, taking the risk that everything would end when it was going so well and the cycle of failed relationships would continue.

One evening as we sat across from each other at a table over cocktails, having pleasant conversation, I asked Jamie about family and learned the normal things—place of birth, number of siblings—things I had never known before we became more than friends.

Then came the unbelievable.

"My mother was killed in a car accident when I was two."

For a moment, I had difficulty absorbing it. My ears rang and Jamie's face blurred as I stared ahead in disbelief. It was the first time I had met another person whose life had been altered by a fatal car accident. That we shared a common tragedy was uncanny and unsettling. It was as if I would never escape it, as the death I accidentally caused would affect every word in every chapter of my life.

Jamie continued the story of a difficult childhood without a mother. I thought as I listened, *I can't tell my story.* Again, I envisioned judgment—my car had slid into the path of another mother and there were other motherless children out there because of me. How could anyone want a relationship with someone who would constantly remind them of their own personal loss?

That night as I drove home, I could not stop my tears. I didn't cry for what I thought was the end of the relationship; I cried because of what I had learned about Jamie's life as a motherless child. My tears were for Jamie and for Tim and Bonnie Sloan.

I resigned to end our relationship the next day. Fresh guilt had risen to the surface and I felt myself shrink behind familiar emotional barriers for protection. I didn't think ending it would be difficult, but when we met again, I instead found myself asking more questions about the accident, thinking that the answers might help me with some questions that had festered for years. Jamie saw that I was openly concerned and empathetic, and shared very personal—and undoubtedly rarely divulged—information.

"I don't remember much about the accident. I know the driver was drunk and went left of center and hit her head on. She died instantly."

The calm voice and carefully spoken words surprised me. I wouldn't have known the death was of a parent if I had been eavesdropping.

"Do you know anything more about the driver?" I asked, my heart hurting.

"I never met him. He served some time in jail but people we knew told us he didn't show any remorse at his sentencing."

"Aren't you angry?"

The composed reply shocked me. "No."

In disbelief, I asked, "How can you not be angry with the drunk driver who killed your mother?"

Unfazed and showing little emotion, Jamie told me that although the accident was unfortunate and life-changing, it and the drunk driver were no longer con stant thoughts. The pain was from the years after, from longing for a mother as a young child and knowing she would never come home.

Stunned by the lack of anger towards the drunk driver when I had expected fury, the thought of telling Jamie my story wiggled free from its bonds.

Maybe I can talk about the crash and we'll be okay, I thought. *Maybe it will all be okay.*

I struggled, but finally shared my story with Jamie. We discussed the irony of meeting another person whom a similar tragedy had touched. I felt cared for and understood as I told the details of the crash. The turning point was palpable—it was the first time, other than with Mary Ann and Patty, I had told someone I truly cared for and felt certain it made no difference. I trusted the feeling that Jamie genuinely cared with no underlying judgments. This was of utmost importance to me.

We had entrusted each other with our secrets, and we went from there.

Self-Help Note: Secrecy and Guilt

I can't tell anyone. Everyone will hate me. I'll lose my friends. No one could ever love me if they knew.

It is not only torturous to feel survivor guilt; it's torturous to even think of sharing those feelings with another person. You may feel, as I did, that you must keep that aspect of yourself hidden, and at all costs. You fear that people will run from you in horror, knowing "what happened." At the same time, you may feel that if you don't share your secret with those you love or with whom you have various interpersonal relationships, that you can never truly be close to anyone.

The logical truth—which is hard to separate from the emotional truth when you suffer from survivor guilt—is that if people care about you, they will not stop doing so if you share your feelings with them. And if they do, they are most certainly not considering their own place among an imperfect humanity and may not be worthy of your love.

I just can't think about this anymore. I need to get my mind off it by doing something else, by getting away.

You may also spend considerable energy trying to keep your guilt from yourself. You might become an artist at deflecting thoughts of the traumatic incident and its resulting survivor guilt, or even minimize the feelings to try to decrease their threat to your emotional well-being. Even so, you may still feel a pervasive sadness, a deep, down-inside-a-well unhappiness that will never go away, no matter how much you push away thoughts, feelings and memories.

Survivor guilt will not "go away" if you ignore it. It will dig down inside you and plant itself, then grow in ways you cannot imagine unless you are living it. You *must* talk to someone who can help.

Chapter 6

From the beginning, my relationship with Jamie seemed good. We had been friends before dating and thus had common friends; we shared interests, and had fun together. Everything about it felt right.

I didn't realize it then, but I know now I could not have felt that contentment with any other person. No other person had lost their mother to a fatal car accident and shared that pain with me, and I believed that made Jamie the only person who would love me without judgment about my past. With that love came some cosmic forgiveness for the role I played in Pat's death. I felt that God had finally tipped His hat in my favor, sending Jamie as a spiritual green light to move ahead with my life and forgive myself. Some part of me also believed that if I could bring Jamie happiness after pain, I could atone for my wrong.

Forgiveness and atonement. Aren't they what every person wants (or should want) when they commit a wrong? I had wanted, for nearly twenty years, to give my heart to Tim and Bonnie Sloan so they could know how deeply sorry I was for their mother's death—for being the other driver and living when she had not. I had wanted to fix what I felt I had broken, if not by waving a magic wand and bringing back Pat, then by serving her children for the rest of my life.

With Jamie came my opportunity to make right with the universe. No one else could give me that.

The relationship brought me peace. I had found a place I belonged, a home. Secure in the knowledge that someone loved me for who I was and despite the crash, I came out from behind the skyscraper I had gradually built around my heart and let myself live.

I later learned that I had found security in re-learning to trust someone, after so many years of not trusting a soul. As Dr. Matsakis states, in *Trust After Trauma*:

> Trauma is about loss, and one of the first casualties of having been traumatized is the capacity to trust [.] Trauma survivors not only lose

39

trust in some of the basic premises that keep people functioning (such as the assumptions of personal invulnerability and that the world is just and fair) but they can also lose trust in people, including themselves.

All I knew then was that I was finally happy. I thought about but did not dwell on the accident and Pat's death with the anguish I had in the past. It was still a closely held secret; I did not speak of it with my friends or family. I put it away in a box on a shelf and only took it out when I was ready and needed to mull over the contents in quiet and solitude. My emotional breakdowns that had come frequently and without warning in the beginning years, and then less so in my twenties, slowed to a near stop. I thought I had it all under control.

*   *   *

I could describe in detail my relationship with Jamie, but for many reasons, I do not feel it is necessary. It is enough to say that based on its beginning, I thought our relationship would last. This feeling, from the heart and mind of a person who had struggled to sustain a relationship, was solid and steadfast.

But it was wrong.

*   *   *

One day I was at work on a normal day doing routine tasks when I received an e-mail message from Jamie in error, meant for another woman. I remember feeling rooted to my seat, my lungs constricted, when I opened the message that started, "Hi, Sweetie," and realized as I read that "Sweetie" was not me, but someone from Jamie's past that had entered our present.

An onlooker would have seen me sitting at my computer, utterly still with a ghastly white face, fingers frozen and eyes fixed on the screen. I felt as if a gaping hole had opened beneath me and then sucked me in and down a winding tunnel. My stomach churned mightily as if I was on a rollercoaster in a harsh descent, and I thought I might be sick on my desk. The ill feeling remained as I left my office and drove the thirty minutes home.

The email was proof in writing that Jamie had betrayed the trust I had at first, delicately, and then, unreservedly, given. Jamie was involved with someone else and I had no idea. Something in my neatly arranged psyche fell off its perch on a shelf. Then all the shelves tumbled down, tearing nails from the walls and walls from the studs.

*   *   *

Immediately, I became a different person. The will I had used to put my grief and heartache where they could no longer harm me disintegrated overnight. The pleasant, outgoing person my friends knew, who rarely showed her feelings and was always there for others in need, disappeared. The hardest part was trying to keep everyone from noticing the change.

Shock sustained me for the first few weeks after Jamie and I split, then it ebbed and internal upheaval flowed. A dam of emotion burst inside me. Sadness and grief erupted from my heart, seeped into my bones. I became the hostage of my tears—they came at will, used unbridled force, assaulted me at length. They were in infinite supply and possessed dogged persistence.

And I raged.

How could Jamie *do* this to me? After everything we had shared and the promises made to one another? The liar!

I made a mental list of everything I hated—that our friendship and commitment had ended with cruelty; that Jamie's disloyalty would smother so many happy memories; that "I'll never lie to you, Connie" was a lie. Perhaps worst of all, I had always treated Jamie with respect and kindness and had expected the same in return.

I steamed, boiled, scalded.

But, as was my custom, I did it in private. I cried in my car, behind my closed office door, at home.

After several weeks of unrelenting anger and tears, I felt beaten. The woman who had finally gained confidence became a formless marionette with no strings to support her movements. I was deflated; my newfound self-esteem and hope for happiness hissed out through the puncture in my heart.

*   *   *

Time passed slowly, as it does when you lose someone you care deeply about. Some moments stood still; some days seemed they would never end. I clawed my way through each one.

Thankfully, the job I loved needed me in it, and that filled some of the painstaking minutes. It forced me out of bed when I wanted to stay there and hide from the world, to function coherently and professionally during at least part of my days. I escaped into my left-brain world, crunching numbers and statistics and analyzing data. Projects at work were the only tasks I could focus on and finish; gone was the motivation I had had for creative pursuits in my personal time.

If only the workday had been twenty-four hours long. Then, there would always have been something to keep my mind in check. But it wasn't, so I found new things to do socially and most involved drinking.

I had always been a social drinker, occasionally sharing happy hours and evenings out with different groups of friends. I decided that happy hour was the best idea—I could go out right from work and not have to come home until it was time to go to bed.

It was perfect. I went out with casual friends who knew nothing about my personal life. There was no emotional requirement. I could just stand there and drink—which I did, at first a few times a week and then, as the summer months stretched on, more often. I came home late, went to sleep, and repeated the steps the next day.

Even sleep was no respite; I thrashed nightly in my sheets and often woke crying.

Anger and sadness returned, refreshed. Their attacks came without warning; I walked around unprotected and ran for cover when they hit so no one around me would see their destruction. Unfortunately, there were times when others saw it.

I was apathetic about everything and too fatigued to care, but after a few months of trial and error I became a virtuoso in the art of the disguise. Mastering the use of a self-created "on-off" switch in my brain, I segregated my emotional havoc from my intellectual routine. With the switch on, so no one would know I was crumbling on the inside, I went to work, saw casual friends and visited with my family. I spoke with acquaintances in the grocery store and clients on the phone and my stylist as she trimmed my hair. I ate cake at office birthday parties and made small talk with my neighbors, all the while wanting to die.

My mother had no idea what was happening in my life because I did not tell her, or let it show when we were together. Even though we were (and are) close—I spent little time with her during this time. I knew my internal switch would not work when I was with her, so I chose to avoid her.

Mary Ann and Patty, both my dear friends for nearly two decades, knew what was happening in my life.

Mary Ann offers this reflection:

> In the twenty years I had known Connie, I had never seen her cry before her split with Jamie. When she told me about it, the tears actually sprang from her eyes, as they do in cartoons. I was shocked and felt terribly helpless at seeing her in such a dire emotional state. We met every three to four weeks, and each time I was terrified to see that she was not feeling better with the passage of time. She handled it horribly, and to me, it seemed that she was getting worse as the weeks passed. She was thin and weary-looking, and had an unnatural fear of being alone. She never wanted to go home, not at the end of our visits and not at the end of her workdays. I worried that she would never be the same. Her pain was unspeakable.

Patty remembers that time this way:

> During this time, I was one of the friends Connie turned to. We had been friends for nearly twenty years at that point and were like sisters. We talked often and saw each other on a regular basis, and I saw that she was devastated and extremely angry at the betrayal. I became very concerned about Connie because she used alcohol to numb her pain. She could not bring herself to go home at night, so she found a new group of friends who were willing to go out with her almost every night.

new the transition to single life would be difficult but I had not anticipated izure by enormous amounts of pain and suffering. My despair was prolonged d profound; it seemed far more intense than pain that comes with a breakup.

It confounded me. Even though it was cruel, I should be able to handle it. I had questioned the relationship at times and always knew I would be fine on my own if things did not work out.

So why this mess? Why was I, a strong woman, completely without control of my emotions? Why, several months later, was I not gradually feeling better and thinking of getting on with my life? Why was I crying every day when I thought there could be no tears left in me?

I had no answers.

Chapter 7

Jamie contacted me and opened the conversation for a possible reconciliation. It was inexplicable that I even considered this because even then I knew I should not spend my life with someone who had betrayed me. I knew it was better that the relationship end. On the other hand, the past weeks had been agonizing and maybe Jamie had made a terrible mistake and deserved a chance to make it right. A friend recommended that we see an objective third party to help sort things out. Jamie was surprisingly on board and so I agreed as well.

It was a big step for me to reach out to an objective third party. I had never believed in the need for psychologists; despite my father's death and the accident, I thought I had always been able to hold it together, just as I had seen everyone in my family do after their emotional crises. I always thought I could work things out on my own.

Our first session with Dr. Samantha Young* was in August. She was soft-spoken and kind, and had a nurturing air. I liked her on sight.

"Tell me what led the two of you here," she said.

Jamie and I spent the next hour talking about the end of our relationship in our own words. It turned out that most of Jamie's words, even to Dr. Young, were untrue. Jamie was lying again and the joint counseling ended after just two sessions.

My individual counseling continued.

*   *   *

Saturday mornings at eight o'clock became mine on Dr. Young's calendar, beginning the week after the final session with Jamie. Grasping for relief, I found some in the

---

a fictitious name

comfort of her modest office with the purple-flowered couches and waist-high shelves full of books and two tiny windows where the east wall met the ceiling.

I held my breath from one session to the next, hoping I would last the week without losing my sanity, longing for the clock to show it was time again to sit in my chosen seat in front of Dr. Young's recliner where she propped her sandaled feet to listen. While I waited for time to pass, I went to work and drank afterward and climbed into bed at eight-thirty in the evening, then did it all again the next day.

At my first solo session, I began by giving Dr. Young the requisite history of my life. I told her about growing up on the farm, and my father's death.

"I was in a fatal car accident when I was sixteen," I said, matter-of-factly.

Dr. Young made some notes and looked up. "Do you mind telling me about it?"

I briefly gave her the facts and glossed over my life from that point, wanting to get back to the subject of the breakup. As she finished writing, I began explaining the all-consuming anger I still felt, even after nearly four months, at Jamie's betrayal. It was easier to do without Jamie sitting there.

"It's not about getting back together," I said, clenching my fists as I spoke. "I made sacrifices to make it work when I was having doubts and all I got in return was lies."

I was off and running, heat rising in my face.

"Jamie's already moved on, like the time we spent together meant nothing. And our friends were supportive at first, but now they think something's wrong with me because I haven't moved on too."

"Did they say that to you?" she asked kindly.

"No, but I can tell. They don't know what to say when they see me upset or crying so they don't say anything. And there's tension if Jamie's name even comes up when I'm with them. It's uncomfortable when I'm with my own friends, and it's Jamie's fault."

"Have you told your friends how you feel about that?"

I clenched my fists so hard my fingernails made marks in my palms. "No, it's not worth it. I'd probably just get more of the same. It's easier just to not see them."

Dr. Young nodded and wrote something in her notes. I continued my heated description of my disappointment in others who I thought cared about me while she listened silently.

"I'm just so angry!" I said unnecessarily. "And if I'm not angry at a given moment, then loneliness nearly kills me. There's never a time when I feel nei-ther."

"I want you to come back next week and tell me more, and the week after that and the following week, until we work through it," she said, standing.

Our hour was up.

*   *   *

My life during those first six months of counseling was an unending cycle of emotions. Anger, grief, sorrow, loneliness—it all consumed me and clouded every moment, preventing me from seeing clearly the world around me, from finding a path out of my misery.

I didn't feel at all better over that time, as one would expect to when they are healing from a breakup. My avoidance of family and friends continued, my drinking worsened, and my frustration at not understanding what was happen-ing to me escalated. No one, especially not me, could understand why I was stuck in a downward spiral.

From Sunday through Friday I lived scared out of my wits, not knowing how to survive what was happening in my mind.

On Sunday, it wasn't so bad because I had just been to a session with Dr. Young. But as the week progressed, I declined. On Monday, I might speak briefly with my mother, who had no idea what was happening in my life. I would try to smile and act normal. Shame would reign-what would she think if she knew? The force would build a ball of tension in my chest that, by Tuesday, would have swelled to the point where I was feeling short of breath. On Wednesday, I might talk to a friend who said she saw Jamie out with friends; anger would flare and burn inside me, insidiously. On Thursday, Mary Ann might call, relieving my wait to see Dr. Young to share my pain. She might listen as I cried and raged, and worry because there was nothing she could do or say to get me through it. On Friday, I would face another weekend alone in my house. I might don my "game face" and meet friends at a bar. Then I would go home, exhausted and emotionally spent, and hide under the covers, praying that something deep inside me would not snap and make me kill myself in spite of what I knew it would do to my family before I made it to the next Saturday morning session.

Then the session would come, and Dr. Young would listen, and I would leave her office thinking I just might make it through the next week.

*   *   *

I think a lot now about what it must have been like then for Mary Ann and Patty. After all, they weren't objective like Dr. Young; they were emotionally invested in me, their friend of over twenty years, and they had never seen me unable to control my emotions.

They must have been terrified.

Mary Ann remembers:

> When Connie and I met in the early months after the breakup, she repeated, "this is not about Jamie, this is not about Jamie", like a mantra. Our visits focused entirely on her pain and she cried for much of the time. It was very draining and I felt helpless because, frankly, I *did* think her pain was about Jamie. What else could it be? Mostly, I listened. I knew that I did not have the skills to help her, and I felt so guilty because she desperately needed answers and I did not have them. She was so alone in her pain. It was heartbreaking.

My visits and talks with Patty were the same. I think now of how worried my two friends must have been when we parted company after they saw me powerless over my emotions and my life. I thank God, though, that they were there, even though there was nothing they could say, no magic wand they could wave to end my sorrow. I did not expect them to heal me. My ailment was too intensely personal, as grief is—a private pain that those closest to the sufferer cannot under stand or diminish. It was enough that they listened and unwittingly saved me from madness.

*   *   *

In February, after I had been seeing Dr. Young for about six months, she tapped a stone that caused a landslide.

The week prior to the session had been particularly difficult. As usual, my therapy high had kicked it off well. But then the rollercoaster crested and plunged me into a black tunnel. At the lowest point, I had to cancel plans with friends because I could not stop crying.

Exhausted, I fell into my usual seat on the couch facing Dr. Young, next to the oak end table with the always-full tissue box. I got right to the point.

"I give up! Maybe everyone *is* right. Maybe this *is* about the breakup and I *am* lost and in denial since Jamie's gone. Maybe everyone's judgments are justified. There, I said it!"

But even when I said it, I didn't believe it. I refused to believe I wasn't strong enough to handle the end of a relationship without falling to tiny pieces.

She looked at me and said, with conviction, "I don't think this is about Jamie."

I was at once relieved and more confused. After several months of therapy, I knew she would not make that statement unless she believed it. It was comforting to hear her confirm what I'd felt for some time. At the same time, I had no idea what could be wrong with me.

"Then what is it?" I asked, exasperated.

"I'm not sure, but we'll figure it out." She seemed determined. "Tell me some more about your childhood."

Where is she going with this? I've told her everything, I thought.

"I had a happy childhood," I replied with a sigh. "We had a loving home and I always felt safe. Other than my dad dying and the accident, my life was wonderful."

She twirled her pen in thought. "Tell me about when your father died and how it was for you."

I pictured my dad as I had seen him when I was young, working on the farm with his shirtsleeves rolled up. "Well, I was sad and it was really hard on my mom and the family, but I was only eight. I didn't really start to understand what it meant nor the finality of it all until a few years later."

She asked me a few more questions about my dad and then said, "Let's talk more about the accident."

To that point, she knew just the facts. I had told her a few details during our first sessions but had not mentioned it since. It had taken so long to put my toxic feelings and thoughts about Pat's death away where they could no longer hurt me; I didn't want to dredge it up. I also didn't think that my purpose in seeing Dr. Young was to feel "better" about it and talking about it would not bring Pat back.

I started to paint the picture of the day for her, my tone factual. "I left for school early one morning. It was chilly and the sun was coming out and I was listening to music. I was just driving. Then before I knew it, I was sliding, and there was this car heading towards me...and then we...we..."

I stopped abruptly as if someone had just punched me in the teeth, my voice catching sharply in my throat. A second passed and then sobs began to shake me. The outburst took control; I was as useless against it as a spoon cutting meat. And I was frightened. I leaned forward in my seat; putting my hands over my head while sobbing uncontrollably.

Dr. Young was concerned, but did not seem surprised at my sudden breakdown. "It's okay, Connie," I heard her say, trying to calm me.

"I-I don't know what's wrong!" I choked.

She did. She spoke softly despite the noise I made, and began to explain what she later told me she had been thinking for a few weeks—that my past was catching up with me, that my pain from the breakup had invited back my pain from the crash.

The thought had not once entered my mind, but there it was.

Realization tore through me like mortar. I thought of my teenage life after the crash, filled with unremitting grief that I tried to drown by drinking. I thought of how I had felt abandoned by those around me in dealing with my grief after the crash. The parallels between my past and present were unmistakable.

I dropped my head in my hands and cried harder. "Oh my God!" I cried. "I can't believe this!"

"It's okay," Dr. Young said again. When I looked up at her, I saw through my tears her face filled with compassion.

"But h-how can this h-happen?" I asked, my shoulders heaving.

Her tone was gentle.

"You never dealt with it, Connie."

It was true. I had pushed it away so it couldn't hurt me anymore and all but buried it when Jamie and I met. It had lain dormant for years, the staggering pain, guilt, emptiness, shame, and monumental lack of self-worth. But like blood from a scar ripped open, it had all exploded to the surface.

Dr. Young continued. "Unresolved trauma-related feelings never go away. They always live inside you, swept up in a neat little pile of dust until something comes along and kicks it and makes a mess of them again."

With her next patient waiting in the hall and our session ten minutes past its end, she said, "I think you have post-traumatic stress disorder, Connie." She stood and gathered me in a warm hug as I tried to get control of my emotions.

Her words were like music, the relief immediate and powerful. I felt comfort in knowing that my complete loss of control over everything in my life was a condition and not a flaw.

My emotional state had a name.

With that, there had to be a way to make it better.

Self-Help Note: Triggers of Past Trauma

"Triggers" are reminders of past experience-something you experience today that reminds you of "yesterday," like a song from decades past that "takes you back" to that time in your life.

For many people who survived a fatal or near-fatal car accident, triggers that remind them of the trauma they suffered could include circumstances similar to those that existed at the time the accident occurred. If the accident occurred while it was raining or snowing, the survivor may have difficulty driving in inclement weather or not be able to drive at all. Even simply driving by the location of the accident may be impossible for survivors. Driving with the windows down past a patch of lilac may even trigger memories of the accident if that scent was in the air when the crash occurred.

But emotions themselves can also trigger the memory of a past trauma. As stated in *Life After Trauma* by Dena Rosenbloom and Mary Beth Williams:

> Feelings can quickly bridge you back to a past experience when you felt a similar emotion. This can leave you feeling puzzled by your strong reaction to a present situation, until you realize the connection to the past. Often, the connection to the past may not be obvious, and at times you may not be able to figure it out right away. The more you learn about your emotions from the trauma, the easier it will become to know when past emotions get triggered into the present. Even a trigger that appears to be small or inconsequential can expand rapidly into the big reservoir of feelings associated with the traumatic memory.

I never could have identified the connection of my feelings to the trauma of my accident. I needed the help of a learned professional to understand the depth of my pain. If, after a trigger or subsequent trauma, you exhibit depression or grief reactions like sadness, crying, and lack of sleep that are pervasive, uncontrollable and last longer than you feel they should, please consult a doctor or psychologist.

Chapter 8

I cried for nearly the entire following week.

I thought of Dr. Young's words—*You have post-traumatic stress disorder.* Though I was tremendously relieved to learn the root of my emotional upheaval, the knowledge brought with it an army of new nightmares; each insight I had into the connections between my past and present was a bullet shot through my heart.

Emotionally spent, I soon turned to educating myself about my diagnosis.

All I knew then about post-traumatic stress disorder (or "PTSD") was that Vietnam veterans often experienced it after they returned from the war. I knew that brave soldiers sometimes buried their visions of war's carnage to survive emotionally, and that those memories sometimes resurfaced with a subsequent trauma. There was a high rate of suicide among these veterans, I had read. Some barely survived, abandoning family, friends and steady jobs for homelessness and alcoholism because trying to live a normal life with the haunting of war was unbearable.

At first, I did not understand how the disorder applied to me, that it could manifest itself in any person who suffers a trauma. I didn't know that it's not confined to the mind of a war veteran and can strike anyone who is abused, was a victim of a violent crime, survived a natural catastrophe, walked away from a fatal car accident, or experienced other serious trauma.

Dr. Young explains:

> History documents the existence of serious distress following trauma for hundreds of years. Categorically defined in 1980 by the American Psychiatric Association as an anxiety disorder after the Vietnam War, post-traumatic stress disorder affects thousands of individuals surviving child and domestic abuse, suicide, rape and other traumas.
>
> According to the APA's *Diagnostic and Statistical Manual of Mental Disorders, Fourth Edition (DSM-IV)*, with PTSD, the patient has experi-

enced or witnessed or was confronted with an unusually traumatic event that both involved actual or threatened death or serious physical injury to the patient or to others, *and* caused the patient intense fear, horror or helplessness. The hallmarks of the disorder are "persistent re-experiencing of the traumatic event, persistent avoidance of stimuli associated with the trauma and numbing of general responsiveness, and persistent symptoms of increased arousal."

After Connie's car accident in 1977, she experienced chronic PTSD, meaning that her symptoms lasted longer than three months; in fact, they lasted close to two years before she unconsciously chose to put them away where they could no longer cause her daily harm. In terms of re-experiencing the event, she had minor flashbacks of the accident. She also experienced intrusive emotions that overwhelmed her when she thought of the accident and its result or when another person mentioned it; this took place during nearly every of her waking moments for an extended period and caused severe psychological damage. The trauma-generated emotions of fear, anger, and anxiety that she felt at being involved in the accident and knowing someone died in it caused, as they do in many patients, a strong physiological reaction that led to hyperarousal symptoms in Connie of irritability, inability to concentrate, explosive outbursts and sleep disturbances—all of which were completely uncharacteristic. If these were not enough, she also suffered from avoidant or numbing symptoms in which she felt completely empty and detached from humanity—she withdrew from friends and family members both physically and emotionally, endured extreme fatigue and apathy, and had little motivation to participate in her normal teenage activities and pursuits.

If these and other symptoms of PTSD go untreated, the damage caused by the disorder can be lasting, even permanent. Unaddressed, PTSD can lead to the related disorders of chronic depression, alcoholism, anxiety and extreme survivor guilt—all of which Connie suffered from immediately following the accident and for several years thereafter, beginning when she was just sixteen years old.

Had the symptoms been recognized and addressed when they initially appeared, there is an excellent chance that Connie would have been able to process a subsequent life trauma as one processes normal grief experiences. Instead, when the later breach of trust in and breakup of significant relationship occurred, it acted as a trigger for Connie's dormant PTSD. The feelings of loss, betrayal, grief and sorrow that she experienced called up painful and unresolved memories from the past and a full-blown onset of PTSD occurred. She began to experience the same symptoms she had nearly twenty years earlier, and found no relief from them in her daily life.

Once I knew even this much about the disorder, a picture began forming in my mind and an understanding of what had been happening to me for nearly half of my life began to emerge. I devoured every bit of information I found about PTSD, learning what it is, what makes some people more susceptible to it than others, who suffers from it, and how it is treated.

I learned that I might have been at risk for the development of PTSD after the accident because of certain factors that might have made me vulnerable to it—had experienced early parental loss, I'm female, and I received poor social support after the accident. Though the presence of those factors does not mean one will develop PTSD, they are indicators. I clearly passed the litmus test—my father died eight years before the accident when I was eight and it was my first experience with the death of a loved one. I am female. Everyone around me avoided talking about the accident almost from the moment it happened. Considering all this after the fact, it did not at all surprise me that I experienced the disorder after Pat died and that the breakup triggered its return.

"How do we treat this?" I asked Dr. Young in the session following my diagnosis.

"For starters, you keep coming here" she replied. "We will get through it together."

I clung to my therapy sessions. Dr. Young's office was the only place I found relief. Though I still socialized frequently with my new friends who knew nothing about my personal life, I rarely saw my closest friends who had been like family to Jamie and me. Most of them had given up trying to understand me. Their lack of support had made me feel unloved and abandoned, and I disconnected myself from that source of pain since there were too many others to manage. With Mary Ann and Patty, I felt like a burden; I knew that my visits with them left them emotionally drained even though they were always supportive and never let on.

And still, not a soul in my family knew how the accident had affected me over the years. None of my siblings knew, and I could not tell my mother.

I had lived so long with shame as my constant companion that it had tainted every thought in my mind. When I considered telling my mother about what was happening to me, I remembered the shame I felt about the crash, about tarnishing (in my mind) my family's good name and causing my mother grief on top of that she had suffered at the loss of her husband. I recalled the strength she showed in her own times of struggle and was ashamed that I could not deal with my own grief in as admirable a way as she.

I withdrew further. I spun a cocoon around my fragile core, self-protection replacing my trust in people and in life. It was only in the presence of my nurturing therapist that I shed my armor.

*   *   *

After my diagnosis, Dr. Young used additional talk therapy to get me to discuss the negative thoughts and beliefs I had created about the crash. She needed to know more about how they had taken over my life, and how the end of my relationship with Jamie had caused them all to resurface, to ascertain the entire landscape of damage she had been called upon to mend. I told her about all the guilt and shame that had consumed me after Pat died, how it had worn me down over the years as nature's elements wear away unprotected wood.

"I still feel so much guilt about living when she didn't," I said. "I always wonder why I didn't die too, and whether I could have done anything to prevent her death. I have thoughts like, 'Why couldn't I have been running late that day?' and 'Why couldn't it have been a day when I picked up my friends for school?' and 'Was there something different I could have done to get control of the car and keep it out of her lane?'"

"Those are normal feelings felt by nearly every single person who experiences death," Dr. Young told me. "It comes from our natural instinct as human beings to think we have control over all aspects of our lives, when we really don't. When some terrible event challenges that assumption, we blame ourselves for not being in control."

"I've told myself over and over that it was an accident," I said.

Dr. Young looked at me kindly. "It *was* an accident, Connie."

"Logically, I know that's true. But it does nothing to make the guilt go away. It never goes away. It was quiet while Jamie and I were together, but it was still there."

"I don't know that it will ever go away," she said. "But I do know that you can talk about it here, and we can look for ways to help you deal with it and put it in perspective. If we do that, we might be able to change your thinking about the role you played in the accident and its outcome."

"I don't think I should feel better about it, if that's what you're saying. If someone else is dead, I don't think I'm supposed to feel better."

"That's normal, too." Dr. Young explained, "Survivor guilt is very complex. On the one hand, we feel terrible that such an awful thing happened to someone else, and on the other, our human instinct for self-preservation fills us with gratitude that we did *not* die. It's a horrible contradiction. We feel hideous that we're happy about living, so we allow ourselves to stay miserable to cancel out the happiness. This is unconscious, of course, but it happens quite often. People who suffer from survivor guilt do not allow themselves to be happy because they feel it would be disrespectful to the memory of those who died."

Hearing this was hard for me to handle, but I felt it to be true. I realized then that until I met Jamie and began to rebuild my self-esteem, I probably believed on some subconscious level that I did not deserve to live a happy life and was completely unworthy of love. It made sense—after all, I had not had success in my dating relationships before Jamie. Jamie, perhaps more because of our shared tragedy than any other connection, returned trust to my life and gave me back my sense of self. Guilt and shame faded into the background of my life—always there, but more subdued—as happiness and peace finally came forth.

Slowly, I was beginning to understand the connections between my crash at sixteen and the end of my love relationship years later. There had been a pattern to my emotional well-being. As a young girl, I trusted people and the world, and felt the safety and security that every human being needs to achieve happiness. The accident stole them from me; Jamie gave them back. At Jamie's betrayal they instantly disappeared again.

Understanding PTSD and its related conditions as the reasons for my rapid emotional descent after the breakup was enlightening, but it did nothing to diminish my psychological relapse. I was right back where I started.

My old friends, Guilt and Shame, returned and they were pissed that I had ignored them for so long. They met up with PTSD, Depression and Anger in a mental maelstrom that did not care about talk therapy.

The storm raged, and I could see no end to its fury. I tried to seek shelter but there was none in sight.

Maybe I am finally getting just what I deserve, I thought.

Self-Help Note: The Clinical Criteria for Post-Traumatic Stress Disorder

The *Diagnostic and Statistical Manual of Mental Disorders, Fourth Edition* lists the criteria that experts use to diagnose an individual with post-traumatic stress disorder. They are as follows:

- Criterion A1&A2: The traumatic event you experience or witness involves "actual or threatened death or serious injury" and you feel "intense fear, helplessness or horror."

- Criterion B: You re-experience the trauma in the form of "recurrent and intrusive recollections of the event or recurrent distressing dreams in which the event is relayed" as well as flashbacks and discomfort or intense distress when you're in situations that remind you of the trauma event (i.e. anniversaries).

- Criterion C: You show "persistent avoidance" of anything that reminds you of the traumatic event and feel numb or disinterested in loved ones, things you cared about in the past, and the world around you.

- Criterion D: You feel "persistent symptoms of increase arousal" such as trouble falling or staying asleep, nightmares, hypervigilance, irritability, outbursts of anger and difficulty concentrating on or completing tasks.

- Criterion E: You experience the symptoms in B, C, and D for at least one month.

- Criterion F: The symptoms have significantly affected your interactions with others, your work performance and/or other important areas of your life.

PTSD can develop either immediately or within six months ("acute PTSD") or as much as months or years later ("delayed-onset PTSD") after a traumatic event. In delayed-onset PTSD, symptoms occur from six months to between 20 and 40 years after the traumatic event.

Chapter 9

By spring, it had been a few months since my therapist had diagnosed me with post-traumatic stress disorder and chronic major depression.

I was waking every day wishing I had not.

I felt like an inmate serving a life sentence in solitary confinement, living in a dark hole thinking every day of my crime. I desperately wanted someone to administer a lethal injection so I could be done with it all.

Though I wanted to die, I knew I could never cause my own death. My mother had been through too much to handle my suicide as well. My dear grandfather, with whom I had a very special relationship, would never recover from it. In the pinhole-sized pocket of my brain that still worked logically, I knew that they and my siblings and friends loved me, and that my own demons would haunt them forever if I killed myself.

I couldn't do it.

But my living during that time was a sort of death. The woman I had been until Jamie left—who was, at times, a woman I did not truly know—was dying. The death was slow and painful, a cancer plucking the healthy cells from my spirit and identity. It was leaving me only with tissue, blood and bone.

I had no idea how I would rebuild the rest.

I continued to research PTSD, wanting to know more about what was killing me. Countless books and articles confirmed for me what Dr. Young had said—that a personal loss or other current life change could call up memories of a trauma. Even though I had not lost Jamie to death, the loss of the relationship and grief were powerful enough to call up memories of my grief over Pat Sloan's death.

It took me back two decades, and I was living it all again.

I was forty but again sixteen, driving down that icy road and losing control of my car, walking the halls of my school feeling either utterly empty inside or overwhelmed by emotion and uncontrollable bouts of crying.

My psychological pendulum swung between the two extremes and I never knew where it would be on any given day.

On one day, I might feel a terrific pounding in my chest, have horribly intrusive and unpredictable thoughts and emotions about Jamie and be uncharacteristi-cally irritable. The next day, I might wake after ample sleep and feel completely exhausted, experience no feeling *at all* in my chest (neither physical nor emo-tional), and feel no connection with my own mother speaking to me from across a table. It was terrifying not to know who I was going to be when I woke up in the morning. It was even more frightening trying to hide who I was each day from the rest of my functioning world.

I learned from Dr. Matsaksis's in-depth writings on PTSD that this is a typical mani-festation of the disorder. In her book, *I Can't Get Over It,* she says:

> Whenever or however you re-experience the trauma, it is usually pure agony. As a result, both emotionally and physically you alternate between being "hyper" and being "numb" or "shut down."

She also explains this concept in her book, *Trust After Trauma*:

> The physiological reactions to trauma, and remembering trauma, encom-pass two seemingly diametrically opposed extremes—hyperarousal and numbing—or overreacting and underreacting. Although on the surface these two reactions seems like opposites, they are interrelated. Prolonged hyperarousal can lead to numbing and some trauma survivors suffer from both hyperarousal and numbing within a short period of time.

Thinking back, I remembered experiencing both hyperarousal and numbing symptoms after the crash. The terror of the situation had aroused biological symptoms—intrusive thoughts about my role in the accident and difficulty con-trolling my emotional responsiveness—at completely unpredictable times during every day. I never really experienced flashbacks and nightmares.

The numbing symptoms had been much worse. I was devoid of feeling, tired and apathetic, and felt utterly detached from people and the world around me. I withdrew from most social interaction.

It was the same for me at forty. I did experience arousal or biological symptoms of PTSD—in fact, the pounding in my chest from a racing heartbeat happened enough that I sought medical attention. Doctors performed an electrocardiogram test and found an abnormality, then ordered me to wear a heart monitor for a brief time to determine whether there was a deeper problem (there was not). And, I experienced intrusive thoughts and emotions that came at will and with force, as if they were being pumped into me with a needle.

But, as in the past, the downer symptoms were worse than the uppers. I literally dragged myself through my days, caring enough about my job to make a decent effort but feeling apathetic about everything else. It was torturous to be around people; no one had been where I was and it seemed ridiculous to have conversations about the weather and what kind of gas mileage my car got and how crowded it was at the mall on Saturday. When I had to be around people, I flipped my psychological "get it together" switch on and tried to be the Connie everyone expected me to be—calm, composed and cheery. It was nothing short of bliss when I could turn it off and run for the cover of my office or car or house and be alone again.

My reading told me that these numbing symptoms went hand in hand with depression, and that PTSD usually teamed up with either depression, anxiety, alcohol abuse or a combination of these related disorders. I was living proof. Depression and alcohol abuse had been the hallmarks of my existence after the accident, and I had fallen back into their arms since the breakup.

I read book after book about symptoms and conditions, about what I had and what had caused it and how I could get better. And I got worse. I could not stop it. I was like a person watching a documentary about lung cancer, nodding in agreement with the narrator as he decries the effects of smoking—while sitting on the couch having a cigarette.

The disorder and its cohorts were winning.

*   *   *

With PTSD's return came the resurgence of my daily thoughts of Pat's family, and the pain of knowing I had changed her children's lives.

I had convinced myself long before that I had ruined their lives, that my role in claiming their mother's life had cursed them with sadness and pain, and I again became obsessed with the need to find out how they had survived their tragedy. I *needed* to know how their lives had turned out. Though I was not sure how, I was ready to give the rest of my own life toward righting any further wrongs they had encountered.

And I still longed to share with them my deep sorrow. I wanted to hold them in a tight embrace and take their pain away—pain I imagined was still flaming bright in the forefront of their lives—though I was an unlikely and probably unwanted source of support.

I began again to visit Pat's grave.

As before, I was anxious—still fearing discovery by her family, even though it had been years since I'd been there and they had never seen my face. On my first trip back, I found her grave to be well-tended; flowers lovingly planted and nurtured as someone cared for her even in death. While I wept over them, I wondered whose hands had dug into the soil and whether they still cried for her. I thought of a similar visit I had made just a few years after the crash and near Christmas, when I had found a small pine tree planted there and decorated with colorful ornaments. It had been a stark reminder that Pat would never again celebrate that or any holiday.

My drive-bys began again, too. I had to see the house Pat had lived in when she died as I had done so many years before. I found the Sloan name still on the mailbox, but now, instead of hoping to find children playing in the yard and trying to be happy, I hoped to see her husband. Visions of him leaving the house filled my mind; I imagined I would see him from my car parked clandestinely down the road and that in his walk I would see he was okay.

A few times, I almost stopped to ask him for unneeded directions, just to satisfy my obsessive need to see that he was all right.

*   *   *

My weekly sessions with Dr. Young continued through the summer and fall. The intensive psychotherapy helped me uncover the connections between the crash and the breakup and delve into the quagmire of my negative belief system.

Despite many discoveries, I still felt out of control, a prisoner of my raging emotions. I drank solely to cope and found it resulted in memory loss. Not only did I have trouble remembering what had happened while I was drinking; I was even forgetting things that took place in sober moments.

Dr. Young had learned more about my drinking habit over the year we'd been doctor and patient and warned me numerous times of the dangers of dependency, but I was unwilling to give up alcohol.

After the first six months of therapy, she had suggested I try an antidepressant drug to help steady my emotions in lieu of drinking to drown them, explaining, as I already knew, that alcohol was a depressant.

"Depression is common in PTSD sufferers, Connie," she said.

"I know. I've read that."

"Do you know what depression is?" she asked rhetorically. "It's not something you can control, as you may think. There's a chemical in the brain called serotonin, which is responsible for feelings of well-being. Sometimes people don't have enough of it. It's no one's fault. It just is."

I just nodded.

"An antidepressant balances out the brain's natural chemicals and may help you feel better over time. There are several on the market and I can give you some information to take to your family doctor, if you think you want to try one."

"No, that's okay. I think I'll be okay," I said without conviction.

A few months later, after she had mentioned it several more times, I agreed and got a prescription for Celexa from my family doctor. I did not get it filled.

I don't know what made me think I could handle things myself—I had been in therapy for a year, was drinking more than when I began therapy, and my mental health was steadily declining.

When our visits began, Dr. Young had used a therapy technique called Eye Movement Desensitization and Reprocessing, or EMDR, to help me reprocess the negative thoughts and feelings I had surrounding the breakup. She explained to me then that she had used it with patients to alleviate distress associated with traumatic memories; she felt it was an appropriate treatment choice in my case because she saw from the beginning that I was suffering from severe emotional distress from the traumatic breach of trust that ended my love relationship. I was reliving the event, as well as my negative perceptions, thoughts and beliefs surrounding the event on a daily basis with no reprieve.

The technique had not magically cured me over the course of my therapy. In the beginning, I had felt temporary relief from crushing distress by the end of individual sessions, but no lasting effect. So, we had set it aside for awhile.

After my PTSD diagnosis, Dr. Young began again to use EMDR with me on days she noticed I had a high level of distress. I knew from my reading that it's sometimes used to treat PTSD, so I acquiesced to trying it again in the hope that on a subconscious level, my mind, knowing what ailed it, would allow EMDR "in" to do its work.

But it didn't.

Dr. Young offers this reflection:

> EMDR is an extremely effective tool for working through the effects of trauma. The beauty of it is that it is "client centered", or "psyche-centered", meaning that the keys to unraveling the entrenched beliefs that are the product of trauma lie within the client, not the therapist. Connie was caught in a deeply held belief system that insisted upon her own suffering as the *only* means she had to make reparation for the death of Patricia Sloan. She feared that letting go of her self-imposed suffering would make her exactly what she feared the Sloan family thought of her—irresponsible and uncaring.
>
> The bottom line is that EMDR cannot dislodge from a person something they do not want to let go; it cannot dissolve what is perceived as the

glue that is holding them together until and unless there is something equally compelling to replace it.

In Connie's case, we did succeed in reducing her anxiety enough for her to get through another day or week. It afforded us the opportunity to sort out the depth of her belief that being happy and feeling good in her life was also an act of abandonment. It led us to the psychological equation that directed her life and the inevitable conclusion that she had to know how those two small children fared without their mother before she could reconsider her attachment to this belief.

Grasping for some relief, I eventually took Dr Young's advice and began taking the antidepressant.

I expected a miracle cure and was disappointed when I did not get it. I took the drug for several weeks but felt no change; the black cloud did not spit me out. I was still in a severe depression, could not concentrate and was easily distracted, had trouble sleeping and cried quite often.

But, I was still drinking alcohol almost daily and in excess.

Dr. Young shared with me that she had spoken with a psychiatrist and a pharmacist about its effectiveness in my case, and that they both had told her, "I she's drinking that much, she might as well not even take an antidepressant."

So, I picked my drug of choice. I threw out the pills.

Self-Help Note: EMDR Defined

EMDR—What is it?

EMDR is a method of psychotherapy designed by Dr. Francine Shapiro in 1987 as a treatment for trauma sufferers. In her book, *EMDR, Eye Movement Desensitization & Reprocessing: The Breakthrough 'Eye Movement' Therapy for Overcoming Anxiety, Stress, and Trauma*, Dr. Shapiro sets forth this treatment whose use has proven effective in decreasing psychological stress in an estimated two million trauma sufferers of all ages.

Her findings are based on her chance personal observation in nature that eye movements can reduce the intensity of disturbing thoughts, under certain conditions. After much research and study, she created a specific process of using rapid eye movements to diffuse the negative feelings that remain when a person experiences a trauma. Research has shown that the brain becomes "stuck" when a person is very upset, and can't process stimulus information as it does normally. It freezes that moment of the trauma so that, for the trauma sufferer, remembering a trauma may feel as bad as going through it the first time.

With EMDR, the goal for the therapist is to help the trauma victim stop reliving negative images, sounds, and feelings when the event comes to mind. Though the sessions begin with a recollection of the traumatic event and can be painful for the victim, the process is designed so that, at the end, the victim still remembers what happened, but it is less upsetting.

More information can be found in Dr. Shapiro's book and on the EMDR International Association's website at www.emdria.org.

Chapter 10

Just after she discovered the link between my past and present, Dr. Young had suggested I begin journaling. She believed strongly in the power of releasing feelings on paper and shared that she had recommended it as therapy to past and current patients on myriad healing journeys. She said it might help me to start to come to terms with the accident and explore my thoughts and emotions about it and the breakup.

I obeyed. I began a journal in early 2002, and I wrote as often as I could, alone and sometimes with a drink in my hand, hoping to see color again in my life. I wrote to give form to my demons, to face them and try to banish them from my world. Nothing was off limits for me on the page; I could unleash a torrent of anger or cry until my tears blurred the words. I didn't have to flip a switch and be someone else for the public. I could be angry with Jamie, miserable for Tim and Bonnie, or unabashedly self-pitying and no one else would see.

I wrote about how I seemed in the middle of the pain—as if the crash had happened that day and I was sitting on my mother's couch as a grown woman numb, watching the well-wishers shuffle across the living room to pat my hand. Questions poured from my pen: *Why did this happen? Why did Pat have to die. Why am I still living? Why didn't I go to the funeral home?*

The following is an entry from June 2002:

> I feel so awful for what happened and for the pain so many people have suffered. I wish they knew the depth of my sorrow. I should have gone to the funeral home. I should have stifled my fears and gone with Mom when she asked. At least I could have told Pat's family how I feel instead of allowing it to fester and drive me mad all these years. What did they think when I wasn't there? That I was too ashamed to show my face? That I have no conscience? Do they think I'm callous and self-interested and unrepentant because I didn't go?

My journal was also where I turned as I struggled to understand what was caus-ing the voices in my head to continue their incessant noise, why I seemed des-tined to listen to them for the rest of my life. It was hard to get my arms around the concept that I had a disorder of the mind—I had always been a strong, self-sufficient person and it was hard to believe it had happened to me. Knowing that others suffered from the same condition made it even harder to understand why no one ever discussed it.

This entry is from later that summer:

> "Mental illness." Why is it so often misunderstood and seldom dis-cussed? Is it really so different from physical illness? People seem to view the two as if they are in no way similar when, in truth, they are. Society, in general, seems ignorant of the fact that events can cause injury to the mind just as they can the body. Cancer's invasion of a body is similar to trauma's invasion of the mind.

> Mental and physical disorders are not so different, so why does society share sympathy and offers of aid when someone has a physical disorder but runs when someone has a disorder of the mind? Why is it accept-able to take painkillers and antibiotics and chemotherapy to alleviate pain and heal from physical ailments, but there's a stigma attached to taking an antidepressant or other drug for an ailment of the mind? Most view pain from a mental injury as a weakness, and judge the depressed at fault for the low serotonin levels in their brain when nature itself is guilty. It should not be this way.

> PTSD is real. It is evil destroying good and it is no longer in remission; the bad cells have resumed production and are killing the healthy ones, once again.

In journaling, I explored at length some issues Dr. Young and I discussed in our brief one-hour sessions. I wrote of things we never discussed at all, things I could never share with any other person. It was awful and gut-wrenching and lonely; it was cathartic and enlightening and calming. Over the next year, it would be my refuge.

*   *   *

One looking at me from the outside but with knowledge of my mental state would have called me an "active depressed" during that time. In other words, I was chronically depressed, but I was *busy*.

In addition to visiting Pat's grave, driving by her former home and writing in my journal according to doctor's orders, that summer I resolved to find out more about the Sloan family and where their lives had taken them.

Dr. Young and I had talked often of survivor guilt. I learned what it does to people like me who walk away from a tragedy that claims another's life. I learned that, though guilt is no longer considered a symptom of PTSD, it is very common among trauma survivors.

As Dr. Matsakis states, in *Trust After Trauma*:

> Survivor guilt hearkens back to atavistic notions about sacrificing to the gods to assure a desired outcome. The idea is that by punishing yourself, you can undo the damage or, at least, keep bad things from happening again.

I now think that part of the reason I created the work of investigating the lives of the Sloan family—other than for the reason that I genuinely cared about whether life had been kinder to them in the long run—was that I *wanted* to feel bad. I felt that if I allowed myself to stop thinking about them or feeling bad about Pat's death, that it would be disrespectful to her memory and her family. I reasoned that I was *supposed* to feel awful forever and did not deserve to be happy, that I was performing a penance for my wrongful deed. I needed Pat's family to be at the forefront of my mind so that maybe my thoughts could protect me from any further harm.

I fixated on learning everything about Pat's loved ones. I wanted to know whether her children still lived in their small hometown or whether they, like me, had moved on and away from their painful past. I wondered whether they had married and had children of their own. Were her parents still living? How had they survived losing a child? Had her husband remarried? Not only did I need thoughts of them with me each day as a form of atonement, I needed something to tell me their lives had gone on, that I had not ruined them.

One day that summer as I visited Pat's grave, a feeling came over me that I needed to know more about her family at that very moment. I stood there crying, looking at her name on the headstone, wondering what I could discreetly do to ease my urgent need to know that they were okay. The only thing that came to mind was that the local library might have something of help, so I dried my tears and got in my car, thankful for a mission to undertake.

I found directions and drove there to see if I could learn anything about her surviving family. There was little information in the books and newspapers I skimmed, but I learned I could find out if Pat's husband, Michael, had remarried if I searched the records at the county courthouse.

I was disappointed to learn that the county courthouse was in a different city; I didn't have time to drive there that day because I had been on the way to another engagement and was short on time. There was barely enough time for me to lock up my emotions and assume a normal appearance, to run through my inner revolving door and change into my superhero attire, before I presented myself in public. It would have to wait.

A few days later, I visited the cemetery again and then drove to the county courthouse. There, after a lengthy search, I found what I was looking for—a marriage license showing that Michael Sloan had remarried nearly seven years after the accident.

With the paper in my hands, I stood for a long while thinking of what this might have meant for Pat's family. I longed to know whether Michael's remarriage had been a good thing for the children, Tim and Bonnie, but was tortured because I knew I would never know the answer. I could imagine what I wanted but imagination was not fact and did not prove to me that something good had come to them.

After some time, I noticed that near the marriage certificates were the death certificates. I paused a moment and then began to scan the books for the correct year. I found the volume dated 1977, opened it, and ran my finger down the alphabetical list to find her name.

I turned to the correct page, and there it was: Patricia Donnelly Sloan's dated and stamped death certificate.

My tears came hard and fast and spilled onto the page, blurring the words but not their truth, and disbelief again overcame me.

Self-Help Note: Writing as Therapy

"Writing, like any form of expression, is healing. Writing about troubled experiences and the troubling aspects of your relationships helps you to see them more clearly and gives you a sense of mastery over the experience."

- excerpted from *Survivor Guilt: A Self-Help Guide* by Aphrodite Matsakis, Ph.D.

A homeless Vietnam veteran, haunted with flashbacks and numbed by post-traumatic stress disorder, decided to join a veteran's writing workshop. At the first workshop, he wrote about a horrific scene from the war. In the following years, he repeatedly discovered that putting past horrors into words helped clear his mind and lift his spirits. "I had to face my demons," he says. "I was an empty shell walking around the street, and writing made me feel like I had a soul."

Souls may be beyond the reach of science, but many researchers echo this veteran's conclusion: Writing about stressful events can be powerfully therapeutic for body and mind.

The Center for Journal Therapy states that, "life-based writing is one of the most reliable and effective ways to heal, change and grow. Your life journal, whether it takes the form of a notebook, computer screen or blank book creates a present-centered between the past and the future.

The power of writing is accessible to anyone who desires self-directed change. It requires no special talent, skills or experience—only a willingness to explore moments of ecstasy and moments of despair, critical illness and crucial life choice, psychological healing and spiritual discovery."

Chapter 11

t soon turned out that journaling, like EMDR, was not enough to help me learn
o cope with PTSD.

√ly depression worsened and my alcohol use became abuse. I drank in excess,
and often alone. The loneliness was overwhelming, as it had been years before. I
continued feeling abandoned by friends who did not understand or know how to
help me, and shame prevented me from reaching out to them and my family.

Dr. Young was particularly concerned, as she had been for some time, about my
drinking. She addressed it often and in a non-threatening and caring way, but it
was clear to me that decreasing my alcohol intake was something she considered of utmost importance in my healing process.

I recall one session in which we had a frank discussion about the use of alcohol
to cope.

As usual, I started by telling her about the week leading up to our meeting—
work had been difficult and it had been a struggle to focus on any task. As usual,
I had fought to avoid the thoughts and emotions associated with my past.

I dealt with it by going out after work and meeting friends," I confessed.

Dr. Young asked me, "How did it make you feel?"

I took a deep breath. "Well, I'm fine when I'm out. I've always been a social
drinker. That's where I spend time with my friends," I replied. "It's usually fun
and it gets my mind off things, which is something I definitely needed this
week."

"What about afterward? How did you feel when you were at work following a
day you went out?"

"It was still difficult to focus as it had been the day before. I guess I felt anxious, but at the same time very depressed. All of the bad things I think about myself were still in my mind and I wanted to break down and cry several times, but I just threw myself into getting my work done and tried not to think about it. Then, I went out again after work that night. I did notice memory loss a few times."

With heartfelt concern, she said, "I know I've said this before, but I'm worried that you may be in danger of developing an alcohol dependency, Connie."

I looked at my hands and felt the tears well up in my eyes. I knew it was true.

She continued, "It's not uncommon for people with PTSD to get to this point, and I can tell you why. The feelings you experience in both the hyperalert and numbing stage of PTSD can be so excruciating that you want to smother them by drinking. If you're anxious, alcohol can calm you, and if you're feeling completely empty, having a drink can liven things up. You have fun with your friends for a few hours and actually feel *something* as opposed to feeling nothing at all. But when you wake up in the morning, your symptoms are still there. The problem is that it becomes a vicious cycle. You feel awful so you drink to feel better, but feeling better is only temporary and your pain still exists. You become desperate and begin to drink more and more until you're on the verge of becoming dependent on something that will only cause further harm to you."

I had read this in every book on PTSD, and I could see that drinking was working against my healing. But it was all I had going for me—it was the only thing that ever made me feel even a bit of relief, a moment of lightness in my world of weight, and I was not ready to make the commitment to stop.

"I want to change it but I just can't right now," I said through my tears.

We had spoken of this before, and Dr. Young was kind. "I understand," she said. "There are stages of change we all go through and you're in a good place. You're thinking about it and that's a start."

I would try—*really* try—over the next year to stop my excessive drinking so that my healing could progress. But I would soon learn that things would get worse before they got better.

        *   *   *

Still upset and crying, I asked Dr. Young, "What do I do now? Every day I feel so low that I think I must be at rock bottom, and then I wake up the next day and feel worse." I paused, but the tears continued. "I'm so lost. Please tell me what to do."

I looked up at her and saw sympathy in her eyes. It was clear that she wanted to give me the answers I sought, just as she had wanted the EMDR to work for me and wanted me to believe that I deserved happiness.

With nowhere else to go, she made a creative suggestion.

"Maybe it would be helpful for you to write a letter to Pat's family," she said calmly.

Her idea startled me.

I wiped a cheek and took a deep breath. "I can't send a letter to them. What would they think? Would it be too painful for them to—"

"Not to send, Connie," she interrupted quietly. "Just to write."

I thought of all the journaling I had done over the last several months, and then I understood.

She continued—"I think it might be a way for you to give your sympathy an outlet. You've been beating yourself up all these years for not having told them personally how sorry you are for what happened, and writing a letter may help you work through that. There could be an awful lot of healing power in seeing your words written in a letter to them."

"I could use some healing power," I said dryly.

She smiled at me. "I know."

I was not opposed to the idea. "So who should I address it to?" I asked.

Dr. Young was pleased that I agreed to do it and we discussed the details in greater depth. Though I wanted to address my letter-that-would-not-be-sent to everyone who ever loved Pat, the plan would be for me to write it to Tim and Bonnie. They were the ones who had lost their mother. In it, I would express my sorrow and grief and tell them that they had been in my thoughts for most of my life and nearly all of theirs.

The plan was for me to work on it a little at a time, stop if it became too painful, and then resume when I felt stronger. When I finished it, I would share it with Dr. Young so that I might feel some sense of peace in having shared it with someone.

I would not send it to Tim and Bonnie Sloan so as not to risk causing them additional undue pain. It would simply be a means for me to try to reach a healed end.

Self-Help Note: The Problem of Substance Abuse

Substance abuse and the development of other addictions are not uncommon for PTSD sufferers. Sometimes the feelings that accompany certain stages of PTSD are so unbearable that the only way to escape them is to drink, abuse drugs, or engage in some other detrimental behavior that takes your mind from the pain. Of course, these behaviors rarely take away the pain for long. They actually increase feelings of desperation and, in turn, one's reliance on the substance. A cycle of abuse forms that, left untreated, can result in significant addiction problems that must be borne in addition to the pain of the trauma itself.

Substance abuse among trauma survivors is a complex issue that has been researched by experts and deserves a much larger treatment than the one I can give in this book. My hope is that the illustration of my own alcohol abuse throughout the story will dissuade you from making the same mistake, or, if you have started down that path, spur you to look for help so you can stop it before it owns you.

Chapter 12

Writing that letter was anything but simple.

It would only be three hundred and thirty-eight words when I finished, but I could barely get through the salutation without losing it. The first sentence took days, the second longer. I put it aside several times because facing the page was as difficult as facing Tim and Bonnie had they appeared at my doorstep.

Instead, in my time away from work—where I could barely focus my attention anyway—I continued my visits to the cemetery and my compulsive search for public information about Pat's life and family.

One day, after a visit to the cemetery, I decided to go back to the library in the Joans' hometown and search for a newspaper article of the accident. After viewing several microfiche tapes, I found an article and cried as I began to read its words:

> A 29-year-old Centerburg woman died from injuries in a two-car accident in Delaware County Friday morning. The patrol said she was driving a Honda Civic south on Ohio 605 when a north-bound Dodge Polara driven by Connie Jo Bachman, 16, of Johnstown slid on ice on the pavement, went left of center and struck the Honda head-on.

I continued to read the rest of the article, wiped the tears from my cheeks, and then went to my own hometown library to look for more. There, the archives yielded an article with a picture of Pat's demolished car and the headline, "Centerburg Woman Killed in Crash."

I stared at it, sick. It was the only time I'd ever seen what Pat's car looked like after the crash, other than when I was at the scene, injured and in shock. I thought of how there had been a person in it before the mangling, and nearly fainted.

By the end of the day, I had accumulated four articles and Pat's obituary. I don't know why I did it. It was just something I needed to do.

I took home what I found and put it with my journal notes and the few sentences of the letter I had mustered. I stared at it all laying there in a pile and prayed to God that He would keep me from ripping wide open at the seams.

*   *   *

In October, I scheduled a routine business trip to a distribution center in Tremont, Pennsylvania. A seven-hour drive in the car seemed appealing, a chance for me to sit in silence with no intruding obligations of normalcy and work through my thoughts and emotions.

As I drove, I tried to figure out what I would say in the letter to Tim and Bonnie, how I would do it without being invasive or dramatic. I spoke potential phrases aloud. I thought of them growing up without their mother as I had without my father. I wondered what all of our lives would have been like without that one day, that one moment, ever having happened.

People on the roads from Columbus to Tremont surely wondered about the sobbing woman driving the midnight blue Toyota Camry on Interstate 70 East that day.

When I arrived hours later at the hotel with puffy eyes and a front seat full of twisted, wet tissues, I started putting my thoughts on paper. I ended the evening having sketched an outline and used a few hundred more tissues.

It was on my mind constantly during the following day as I conducted business and I was thankful to finish and return to my hotel room to type the full letter.

It read like this:

> *"One of the hardest things in life is having words in your heart that you cannot utter."*
>
> *James Earl Jones*

Dear Timothy and Bonnie,

This may be a very difficult letter to read, and I assure you, it is very difficult to write. My name is Connie and I was involved in the car accident that took your mother's life.

Words cannot begin to express the sorrow I feel and have felt for so many years. In a matter of seconds, life for so many was disrupted, never to be the same again. A day does not go by that I do not think about the accident and wonder why it had to happen. And a day does not go by that I do not wonder how you are doing and how you have managed to survive such a traumatic event. I have wanted to tell you these things for many years, but decided not to contact you for fear that it may open tender wounds and cause your pain to surface.

I have come to realize that my pain and sorrow associated with this horrific incident has affected and continues to affect my life in many ways. Although the situation seemed out of my control, I continue to feel enormous amounts of guilt and grief. Finally, after all of these years, I am seeking professional help to work through my bottled up and painful emotions. It is with the support of my therapist that I finally have the strength to share with you how very sorry I am about your loss. I continue to hope and pray that you have found the needed strength and courage to survive this trauma in a healthy and positive way.

I hope I have done the right thing to share with you how much I think about you and your family and I hope that this letter brings you only comfort and no pain. With all my heart, I wish for you a peaceful and happy life.

With sorrow and respect,

Connie Bachman

e following day I returned to the peace and thoughtful quiet of my car for the ve home, thankful for another reprieve from the rest of humanity.

*   *   *

I had traveled the route to and from Tremont for business so many times in the past that I was sure I could do it in my sleep.

On the way home, it was as if I *had* been sleeping behind the wheel. After driving for hours engrossed in my thoughts, I became aware that the turnpike was ending and I had missed my exit hundreds of miles back. I had no idea where I was. Time had completely escaped me, and my left-brain mind, always savvy with directions and logistics, had failed me.

I drove to the next rest area to figure out my location and plot the best way home since I had driven hours out of my way. Newly oriented, I drove back to the highway and my new route home, but my directional mind turned off again almost immediately. I slipped back into a thoughtful trance and lost my way a second time. When I came out of my haze, I realized I needed to get it together and make it home safely and with no other detours.

Again, I pulled off the road to see where I was. When I stopped, I saw a sign that told me I was only a few miles from the object of my thoughts.

I had unconsciously driven completely out of my way and ended up near Pat's hometown of Medina, Ohio.

I sat in my car at the stop sign on the lonely country road for several minutes debating whether I should turn and go home or follow the signs to Medina. My eyes welled up with tears as I pushed down the gas pedal and began the drive to the little town where Pat had lived. *I'll see if I can find out anything else about her family*, I thought. I thought I might find another article at the library about the accident, but I certainly did not plan to find more.

The road I traveled into the town was a main road; everything there seemed to be located on it or visible from it, including the local high school. As I passed it I thought of what I had learned about Pat from my research. *That's where she went to school*, I thought. I had learned her maiden name, too. In a second and without thinking I was turning the car around and heading toward it. Then I was parking in the lot and stepping from my car, my heart pounding.

As I walked through the door, I thought of her hand pulling it open hundreds of times when she was young, carefree and alive. As I stepped across the threshold I wondered what she had been like then, what activities she had enjoyed. I wanted to know about *her*, not just statistics from newspaper articles about the crash and facts from her obituary. I wanted to know more about her as a person—what she liked and disliked, what made her real.

The school library proved a fruitful source of information. Through old school newspapers, I found an article that said Pat had been a cheerleader and a member of the National Swim Team. *She was an athlete, like me,* I thought. As I cried, I wondered whether, had we been the same age, we would have been friends.

Clutching the article in my hands for several long minutes, a thought began to form in my mind.

They have school yearbooks here. What if there is a picture of her, too?

There had been no picture in her obituary or in any of the newspaper clippings I had found, and I did not see any pictures her family may have brought to her funeral. I had no idea what she looked like, only a vision of her wearing a flip or a bun in her hair and eyeglasses shaped like cat's eyes as my older sister and other girls did in the sixties. Yet there I was, standing in the middle of a room that probably had not just one, but many pictures of the former cheerleader and swimmer. I knew I was unprepared for the ramifications of attaching her name to her face, but I also knew I had to see her.

With trembling hands, I continued searching the newspapers and then moved to the Medina High School yearbooks from 1963 to 1966. I turned page after page of pictures of girls with perfectly coiffed and flipped hair or long straight hair with a part in the middle, and of clean-cut boys with pencil-thin ties and bushy-haired boys with long sideburns.

Then, finally, there was Pat, staring up at me. There was the person traveling in the other car that awful day, whose life had ended when she was not yet thirty.

I had finally found her.

I sat there transfixed by her face, tears clouding my eyes, emotion threatening to erupt as I struggled to contain it in the quiet library. I had a picture of Pat, and she looked nothing like my vision of her. She had neither the flipped hair nor the cat glasses and looked more like the athlete that the school newspapers said she had been, her brownish-blond hair cropped smartly to her neck, her face fresh and nearly free of makeup. She looked so unlike the times that it was as if she could have been in my own high school class thirteen years later, perhaps playing on the same basketball team as me and running in the same circles. I got a strange feeling that I had found a lost friend who had always been part of me.

Even more startling than finding Pat's picture when I least expected and feeling a bizarre connection to her was that—after I realized I was not seeing things from vision blurred by tears—I was looking at a picture of a dead girl who could have been my twin.

*   *   *

I eventually made a copy of the photograph and left for home. During the drive, I frequently glanced down on the seat next to me at the article, then the picture, and cried. When I arrived home, the ache in my heart was so dull that I could not bear to be alone. I joined some friends for a night out, thinking it would make me feel better to be around people.

It was strange though, to have gone through a day like that one, then be out with friends and not mention a word of it. I realized how tired I had grown of living alone with it all; how weary I was of turning on my social self as if nothing was amiss; how exhausted I was from trying to survive a normal night out without collapsing under my emotional weight.

Seeing Pat's face deepened the hole of my despair when I did not think it was possible. My mental capabilities deteriorated further; I found myself nearly mentioning to my friends, several times that night, "I met a girl today who looks just like me. I can't wait for you to meet her."

Even without the alcohol, I was mentally disjointed that night. I'm sure I was the loneliest I have ever been, in a room full of friends, my mind not even keeping company with my own body. But I kept taking my liquid medication anyway, because the only other thing worth doing was dying.

*   *   *

Mercifully, the few days between my return from the business trip and my next session with Dr. Young elapsed quickly. I was grateful to return to that nurturing place to feel hopeful, for at least an hour, that someone could help me out of the deep, dank well that had swallowed me. My spirits had lifted some since she had suggested I write the letter to Tim and Bonnie, and at our last visit, I had been almost upbeat about the task before me. I'm sure she was surprised to find me so low again.

I started by sharing the letter I had written to Tim and Bonnie, and watched her as she read, feeling relieved that *someone* had, even if it hadn't been one of the theoretical recipients.

Then I handed her the newspaper articles and Pat's high school yearbook photograph.

Dr. Young looked at the picture and then quickly up at me.

"She looks like you," she said immediately.

"I know," I said, clasping and unclasping my hands around my empty coffee cup for support. "I wasn't quite ready for that, and still don't think I am."

I told her what I could about the experience of finding it on the meandering trip home from Pennsylvania, but it was hard to relive it when I was still trying to comprehend it. We discussed the letter instead.

"How do you feel about it?" she asked.

"I'm glad I'm finished writing it," I replied.

She smiled. "And how do you feel about what you wrote?"

"I feel honest. It was emotional for me but what I wrote is how I feel. But I don't think it's having the effect we had hoped for."

"What do you mean?" she asked.

"Well, though it was helpful to write it, Tim and Bonnie still don't know how I feel. To this day, they probably think I was just some scared kid who ran away from her past and either forgot about it or tries to never think about it."

"Are you saying you want to send it to them?"

"I don't know what I'm saying. Maybe I do. I just want them to know." I paused a moment, confused. "But I know if I send it, it could stir up pain that they've already dealt with and completely disrupt their lives. It wouldn't be right."

We continued to discuss all the reasons I should not send the letter, and by the end of the session, we decided to stick with our original plan.

I no longer liked that plan. And I didn't like the thought that Tim and Bonnie might be out there thinking that the other driver had walked away without another thought of their mother, forever.

Chapter 13

Fall became winter and winter became spring. It had been two years since my PTSD was triggered and there was no relief from my pain in sight.

My frustration was at its peak. Other than quitting drinking, I had tried everything to feel better and didn't know where to turn. I began to wonder if there was a healing path for me at all; my efforts to escape the suffocating grief and guilt had only made me feel worse. Self-pity and negative thinking reigned—I thought misery was my new life, that I was getting the punishment I had deserved for twenty-five years.

Infrequently, a brief ray of hope that I would overcome the disorder peeked through the dark clouds that hung over me each day. Those times, I thought I could find a way to contain my emotions, prevent my violent mood swings and stop self-berating.

Other times I would think, *I'll just try to push all this back into a dormant place, like it was when I was with Jamie.* Of course, I knew that would get me nowhere, but facing it all sure was not healing me. I longed for relief and time brought none of the proverbial healing of the wounds, only further decline.

Now and then, the thought of sending Tim and Bonnie the letter crept back into my mind, but I always dismissed it for the reasons Dr. Young and I had discussed. I simply did not want to cause them any further pain.

Even though I could see the logic in what Dr. Young told me—that the crash in a split second of time should not prevent me from being happy—I felt I could not allow myself that privilege.

"Why do I continue to feel this way?" I asked during one session.

"Because something happened to your belief system slowly, over many years," she answered. "It happens to many survivors of trauma when they have no help dealing with what's happened to them. When no one helped you deal with Pat's death, you began to think it was because you had done something so terrible that no one could speak of it. That led you to form the belief that you are unworthy of happiness and love and deserved punishment."

I found this confirmation of her statement in Dr. Matsakis's *Trust After Trauma:*

> People who have been traumatized, but are lovingly embraced subsequently by their families or others, are much less likely to develop severe or long-term traumatic reactions than traumatized people who are subsequently rejected or ignored by important others (Shay 1994). *** Many feelings of rejection stem from what is called secondary wounding. *Secondary wounding* occurs when the people, institutions, caregivers and others to whom the survivor turns for emotional [...] assistance respond in a way that further injures the survivor.

This "secondary wounding" had caused me, as it does many trauma survivors, to believe that I was a bad person who had done a bad thing and deserved the worst to happen as payback. I had believed this for so long—even though it was not a conscious thought—that I was not sure I could ever reprogram my thinking.

Dr. Young agreed that reprogramming is difficult. "It's easier to change your thoughts than change a belief," she said.

It was true. Despite that, logically, I *thought* I should not let the accident take future happiness from me, it was a built-in *belief* that it should.

As stated in *Life After Trauma* by Dana Rosenbloom and Mary Beth Williams:

> Once we formed our core beliefs, we usually stop thinking much about them. They become a natural part of who we are and how we function. We tend to act on them automatically, as reflex.

Dr. Young had been trying to help me reprogram my core beliefs during eighteen months of intensive psychotherapy. Something inside me was preventing her efforts from working.

I was falling apart because of it.

My friend, Patty, offers the following reflection about what she observed in me during this time:

> I was extremely worried about Connie at this time. There were times we spoke and I knew she was in a very bad place. The sound of the pain in her voice then is indescribable. I called often to check on her, and there were a few times when I could not reach her and it was hard not to panic.

> Her drinking was very much out of control. She never said it, but I knew she did not care if she lived or died. It was obvious to me that she felt she had nothing to live for.

> There were times when I thought she might not survive this period. I was helpless and scared to death for my friend. I tried in vain to reason with her, to tell her that what happened long ago was not her fault. We talked often about what it would feel like to get on the other side of all this, but she did not believe it was possible. Eventually, *I* began to wonder whether it was possible. For a long time, Connie had absolutely no hope.

My emotional state was at its most unpredictable and I began not to know if my functioning switch would work when I called upon it. I frequently broke into tears at the smallest provocation, usually without warning. I could not be with others, and I could not be alone.

Perhaps worst of all was that I felt God had deserted me in my time of deepest need. Mary Ann remembers it this way:

> I have always thought of Connie as a religious person. When we were younger and first became roommates, she would meet her mother and grandfather for church and breakfast every Sunday. She used to tell me how much she loved sunrise services at her church at Easter. Connie and her family's solid relationship with God always won my respect and admiration.

> I knew something was very, very wrong when Connie said she was no longer sure she believed in God, and told me, "If there is a God, I think He has abandoned me." I feared, at that point, that Connie would never recover.

I shared Mary Ann's fears, and I was terrified.

One day, unable to handle the loneliness of my empty home and too emotionally unstable to be around others, I drove around for some time, crying. I cried for everyone who had hurt because of me, for myself, and for the utter waste of Pat's and my lives.

I had planned to meet a friend later in the evening, but I had hours until then and I couldn't get myself together. Eventually, I stopped at our intended meeting place, knowing I would be alone for some time before she arrived. I had a drink, and wrote the following:

> Summer 2003
>
> No one can begin to understand this horrible and debilitating disorder and the pain it causes. It's foreign unless you live there, in the midst of it. It's like not being able to explain to a person from a hot climate the sensation of frigid weather; they have to walk into a snowstorm, feel their eyes water in the blistering wind and their toes tingle with pain and then go numb, in order to comprehend.
>
> This disorder is beyond the comprehension of most unless they live it. It brings incredibly strong swings of emotions, many times without any identifiable cause. Intrusive thoughts assault without warning, smothering all normal thoughts that existed only moments before. Pain comes at will. All logic is gone. Nothing makes sense and even if it seems to for a moment, emotion takes over and wipes out rational thought. It's a nightmare of living the most emotionally tortured time in my life—filled with extreme sadness, intense anger, and blinding irrationality—every day without pause.
>
> No matter what I do or how hard I try to do the right things to overcome it, nothing seems to work. And just when I think I might be making some progress, gaining a slight bit of control over my life and feeling a sliver of relief, I turn the corner and the black cloud sucks me in again. The setbacks are getting harder, and this one seems the worst. I'm exhausted, so tired of the condemning voices in my head. I would rather die than live my life like this. A coward's thought? Perhaps. But my strength is gone and logic lost, and without the two, I have no desire to continue or optimism for a positive future.

I know it was an accident! I didn't intend it and the judge agreed I wasn't negligent. I've heard all the explanations—that we were both in the wrong place at the wrong time, that the accident was part of God's plan for us both. I know how fortunate I am to have a beautiful home, a satisfying job, a wonderful family and great friends. My blessings are rich, as my friends often remind me, and when I can see clearly through the fog, I am humbled with thanks.

But gratefulness fades into the background with a disorder that has a mind of its own. Blessings do not matter when the guilt and sadness consume me. They rear back on their scaly hind legs and breathe roaring fire, blasting me for feeling at ease even for a moment with any fortune or happiness in life. They tell me it is selfish and wrong to enjoy anything in life. How can I, knowing that my accident took the life of another? This is my struggle, every hour of every day.

I wish someone could shake me violently, snapping me into the person I want to be. But the wounds run too deep to heal with gauze and tape. Reality for an anorexic is that they're fat when they're really thin; for an obsessive-compulsive that the doors are unlocked when they're locked. They can't be shaken and cured. Their disorders, like mine, cause them to see things very differently, to live in different worlds.

I'm tired of this world, the one full of guilt and pain that has taken me and my life hostage.

As I finished the last word, I dropped my pen on the table as if it had zapped me with electricity. It terrified me that I had just wondered whether killing myself was such a bad idea after all.

I did not want to die. The problem was, I didn't want to live that way any longer, either.

Still crying, I took out my phone and slowly pressed the digits of my friend's phone number. I asked her to come earlier than planned. She did. We had a drink together and she listened, her face clouded with worry, while I talked and cried.

Then I got in my car and drove home.

*   *   *

I met with Dr. Young a few days after this journal entry. These are her recollections from that time:

> When Connie shared her journal entry with me, my first thought, from a human perspective, was that she was clearly living her darkest hours. My second, from a clinical perspective, was that there seemed a glimmer of hope for a new beginning.
>
> Therapy can be a treacherous path because it often leads us to our greatest self-deception before it uncovers the larger truths that can set us free. For Connie, the self-deception she nurtured was that her own suffering was the only way to make amends for Pat Sloan's death and honor the lives of the children she left behind. Her journal entry marked the moment of greatest tension between the "old" path—her entrenched belief system that justified her existence—and a possible new path that would lead into self-acceptance, forgiveness, and liberation from suffering.
>
> It was difficult to watch Connie in the throes of that change. Her loyalty to her twenty-five year-old creed of suffering was unshakeable because she felt it would betray Pat, Tim and Bonnie; however, so was her determination to meet self-love. The problem was that her alcohol use and self-doubt were running amuck with her native life force and intelligent engagement with the world.
>
> As a therapist, there are times when all you can extend is your compassion and your conviction that profound change is possible. And hope.
>
> This was one of those times.

Self-Help Note: Suicide Warning Signs

During my recovery, there were many times I wanted to just not wake up; it would have been far easier than opening my eyes each morning to find I was still in my own head. But for me, suicide was not a serious option. I did not want to die—I wanted to live, but I wanted to live free of the pain, grief and despairing loneliness.

For others, suicide is an option, and the importance of noticing the signs cannot be overstated.

The following is excerpted from the National Suicide Prevention Lifeline website at www.suicidepreventionlifeline.org:

Suicide Warning Signs

"Seek help as soon as possible by contacting a mental health professional or by calling the National Suicide Prevention Lifeline at 1-800-273-TALK for a referral should you hear or see someone you know exhibiting any of the following signs:

- Threatening to hurt or kill oneself or talking about wanting to hurt or kill oneself
- Looking for ways to kill oneself by seeking access to firearms, available pills, or other means
- Talking or writing about death, dying, or suicide when these actions are out of the ordinary for the person
- Feeling hopeless
- Feeling rage or uncontrolled anger or seeking revenge
- Acting reckless or engaging in risky activities-seemingly without thinking
- Feeling trapped-like there's no way out
- Increasing alcohol or drug use
- Withdrawing from friends, family, and society
- Feeling anxious, agitated, or unable to sleep or sleeping all the time
- Experiencing dramatic mood changes
- Seeing no reason for living or having no sense of purpose in life."

It could be that the PTSD victim really does have no desire to die—that, like me, they just want the horrible cycle of PTSD to end. But in either case, recognition of the signs is vital to helping the PTSD sufferer get the help they need to regain their sense of self-worth and start down the healing path.

Part III—Hope

Chapter 14

Weeks ticked by with no change. I walked around numb, my fragile emotional core exposed. I needed an outlet for my feelings and the need to tell the Sloan family how I felt about their loss was at an all-time high.

At a session with Dr. Young that fall, I hesitantly brought up the idea of sending the letter.

"Maybe we should talk about the pros and cons again first," she said.

We had had similar discussions in the past and I had gotten the impression that, though she tried to be objective, she was not in favor it. I knew her well enough by then to read how she felt about something, even when she was trying to withhold her opinion. I trusted her instincts, but I knew she would allow me to make the decision because she always did.

I began by telling her why I wanted to do it.

"Well," I said, taking a deep breath, "I struggle with whether it would be just a self-ish attempt for relief, or whether it might bring some comfort to all of us. On the comfort side, I would hope it would make Pat's family feel better knowing that I didn't just walk away and never think about her again. And, maybe it would answer for them the question of what I've been doing for the last twenty-five years when they've been living without her."

Dr. Young nodded and let me continue spilling what was in my mind.

"It's such a scary unknown, though. I mean, wondering how they would feel to read this letter is like wondering, when I was sixteen, how they would feel if I didn't go to the funeral home and wondering all these years how they would feel if they found me at the cemetery. I've thought about this since we first talked about writing the letter and I just can't figure it out."

I talked on.

"Is it fair to them? What if Tim and Bonnie have dealt with it the best they can, or worse, what if they haven't dealt with it? Then I'm responsible for hurting them twice."

"There are other questions, too," she said.

"I know. I've been thinking of them."

I told her all the things that had been on my mind constantly since the idea of sending the letter began to crowd out everything else in my head. I rambled about whether to send it, to whom to send it. Should I send it to her husband, now in his sixties and remarried nearly twenty years? To her mother, now nearly eighty and the probable caretaker of her grave? If I sent it to Tim and Bonnie, where would I send it? Did they still live near the small town where the crash happened? How would they react when they got a letter like this in their daily mail, without warning, along with the telephone bill and the direct mail pieces for satellite television service?

"That just doesn't seem like the right thing to do," I said to Dr. Young. "Maybe I could leave them at the cemetery the next time I go. I almost left it there the last time I visited. I just sat there, crying, wishing God would just tell me the right thing to do."

Dr. Young just listened.

I looked down at my hands. "I planted a little flower there that day, instead," I told her. "It was so small I don't think anyone would have noticed it. It was the first time I've left anything there even though I've always wanted to give her something. And when I planted it, I still was looking over my shoulder, afraid someone would see me do it."

I paused and looked up. "Anyway, I know someone still visits because Pat's grave is always well kept. Do you think it would be less invasive to leave the letter at her grave?"

Dr. Young held my gaze for a moment before answering. I saw in her eyes a motherly concern. "Those aren't the 'other questions' I was referring to," she responded.

"What do you mean?"

She took a deep breath and said with quiet firmness, "I want you to think about the effect that sending the letters, whether to Tim and Bonnie only or to the whole family, will have on *you.*"

At that moment, I realized that her tacit disapproval of sending the letter came from looking at it from a different angle—from the view of protecting me. Although she was concerned about the family, she was more concerned about how I would handle their response, or worse, no response at all. It was something I had not given much consideration.

"What if you don't get a response?" she asked me. The odds were quite good that they would not reply—they didn't know me, I hadn't come to the funeral home, it may be too painful for them to dig through piles of aged grief. It may be easier for them not to think about me at all.

"I think I would be okay with that," I said. "The main reason for sending it is to tell Pat's family, mainly her kids, that I'm sorry for what happened and that I didn't just walk away without caring. I sometimes feel like I blew it by not going to the funeral home, and for whatever reason, I need them to know that I care and always have cared. I can do this in the letter. I don't need a response."

I sounded more confident than I felt.

"But you're also very concerned about how her kids have fared in their lives and if they don't respond to you, you still won't know," Dr. Young replied. "Will you be able to handle that?"

"I think I will," I said. "I know that their father remarried and I can only hope having a stepmother helped Tim and Bonnie."

"Okay. Then let's think about this scenario," she said, her tone of voice more grave. "What happens if you get an angry response, one so angry that it confirms the fears and negative beliefs you've had for all these years? What do we do then?"

I didn't know the answer to that question. Could I handle that, at my current level of emotional instability? Would that be enough to push me over the edge I had been teetering on for so many months?

I honestly thought it could not get much worse for me emotionally—I had left sea level a year earlier and taken a nose dive for the bottom of the ocean, where I'd been ever since. Since I felt I could only move up from there, I said, somewhat boldly, "Well, I guess we'd have to figure out a way to get through it."

At least they would finally know my sorrow for their loss, I thought. *And that is something they need to know.*

At the end of the session, Dr. Young knew I was serious about communicating my sorrow to the Sloan family in reality, not just theory. After months of consideration, we decided it was time to explore the best way for that to happen.

*   *   *

During our next several Saturday morning sessions, we discussed how to deliver the letters.

I decided I was not keen on the regular mail service or leaving them at the cemetery ideas. I couldn't imagine how I would feel if some stranger from my traumatic past showed up on my front doorstep, so I knew I couldn't do that to Tim and Bonnie. None of these methods felt right, and I wanted to do something monumental—at least something *I* considered monumental—the right way.

Dr. Young suggested we find a mediator, like a minister or pastor or priest, for assistance. Assuming that Pat's family had and still attended church, we thought we could contact a church leader and seek their advice. Perhaps church leader would be willing to share basic information about the family once we explained my position. Dr. Young even hoped that, after hearing my story they would even offer to deliver the letter, acting as the mediator I desperately sought to help me convey my sorrow.

Since this option was the first viable one we found, we decided to pursue it.

The first part was up to me. Since I had been searching for information about the Sloan family for some time, Dr. Young charged me with finding which church, if any, in the Village of Centerburg, Ohio the Sloan family attended.

As I began my work, I felt a new purpose, and hope where none had been for such a long time. Even though I knew the potential negatives—we would find no one through a search of churches, I would never find them, or, if I did find them, it might cause me more pain—it felt better to be moving ahead in some small way. I would deal with the bad things if, and when, they happened.

All I knew was that Pat's widowed husband, Michael, still lived in Centerburg in the same house he had lived with Pat and the children before she died, and where Tim and Bonnie grew up. I tried to track him through church membership directories on the Internet, but had no luck.

All I could do was create a list of churches in the area with contact information. There were seven churches in all. I reviewed the list with Dr. Young and gave her written permission to make calls for me. Soon, she had called every church listed and left a brief message with each explaining who we were. She requested a return call from each, and as the days passed with the situation in her hands, I prayed someone—the right one—would honor the request.

I sat on the sidelines, waiting. My mind, accustomed to constant musings, wondered and worried. What if the family doesn't belong to a church? What if they belong to a church I didn't list? What if we find the right church but the pastor does not want to be involved with this complex situation, or insists that we leave the family in peace and avoid resurrecting painful memories? There was no news of anything for some time. While I waited, my negative belief system kicked in and convinced me that saying "I'm sorry" was not meant to be and I deserved to live forever with my unspoken sorrow.

Long days passed. Some church clergy returned calls over time with no information; some did not call back at all. When it looked like the plan wasn't working, Dr. Young and I began discussing other options, none of which either of us favored. The search occupied most of my waking and sleeping thoughts; paying attention to anything other than watching the phone was nearly impossible.

Then one day while I was at work, trying to focus and accomplish something in my day, Dr. Young called.

I heard her inhale deeply. Then she said, "Well, Ms. Bachman, we have a hit."

My heart pounded so hard it rattled my rib cage. I said slowly, "Go on."

She explained to me what had happened. "I just spoke with a Reverend Williams from a church on the list you gave me. He was very reserved and at first unwilling to give me any information. But as I shared more about you, he opened up a bit. Eventually, he told me that he thinks Pat's son is a member of his church. I told him Tim would be in his early thirties. He said that's the age of the young man who attends his services."

"What does this mean?" I asked. I wrung my hands to keep them from shaking.

"Well, even after he said what he did, I could tell he was protective of Tim's privacy. I told him that we were at the point of wanting to make contact with the family, and that the decision was not made quickly but over the course of many months and after looking at all other options. He seemed a bit cautious about becoming involved with something this serious. I told him that we would respect the way he chose to handle the situation. He asked me for a few days to digest what I said, and said he would call me back next week."

I said goodbye and hung up the phone, then sat in my office, immobile, for a long time. My heart rate stayed at racing speed for several minutes as I tried to process how close we were to potential contact with one of Pat's children. The fact that someone who knew Tim had returned a call was overwhelming in itself.

I could not concentrate on anything for the rest of the work day, and surviving the anticipation of the next few days until the minister called back was hard. There was the possibility that he would call and say he didn't want to be involved, in which case Dr. Young and I would need to formulate a different plan. There were doubts in my mind too—I kept asking myself whether this was the right thing to do or whether it was an act of selfishness. I considered changing my mind about pursuing the connection so as not to cause further damage.

But I didn't. I still felt it was right.

A few days later, Dr. Young called me at work again.

"Do you have a moment?" she asked.

I got up to close my office door. "Absolutely," I said. I was scared speechless; my heart started its now-familiar dance of anticipation.

"Well...Reverend Williams just called."

"Okay..."

"Tim was at church this past Sunday. He happened to be one of the last people leaving the church so the reverend asked if he could stay for a moment. He told Tim about my call and our conversation. Tim had a response."

I was sure Dr. Young could hear my heart beating through the phone I held at my ear.

"Tim had a response," I repeated.

"Yes," she said. "He said, 'Sure, I would be happy to meet with her. I don't remember much about it. I was only seven. But I'll meet with her.'"

Oh my God, I can't believe this! Oh my God! I thought.

I had been expecting a call from Reverend Williams to help us determine our next move in sending the letter, if we were even to pursue one. I had no idea that the minister would discuss it directly with Tim. And I certainly had not imagined that a child of Pat's would agree to *meet with me*.

"He agreed to meet with me?" I asked, my voice wavering. "But, I just wanted to give him a letter, somehow."

"He said he would be happy to meet with you," repeated Dr. Young gently.

I couldn't speak. The thought of being in the presence of Timothy Sloan was mind-boggling. I thought of Pat's picture and the way a young man with her features would look, and it gave me a jolt. I thought of myself, standing in front of him, stammering—or worse, breaking down emotionally.

I thought maybe, if that was his response, he *wouldn't* hate me.

In disbelief, I picked up a pen and wrote down Tim's words on a tablet on my desk, my eyes filling with tears as my hand moved across the page.

Dr. Young paused for a moment, letting me absorb it. Then she asked, "How do you feel?"

"Um, overwhelmed with emotion. Very scared," I said nervously. "Very scared and not sure what to do next."

"Well, Tim gave his cell phone number to Reverend Williams and said that we could give him a call," she said.

"We? I don't think I can do that." Sobs welled up in my chest. "We, meaning you?" I asked.

She gave a little laugh and offered to make the call. I hung up and stared at the words written on my tablet, *Sure, I would be happy to meet with her.*

I sat at my desk and cried. They were still tears of anguish, but this time they were tinged with hope.

Chapter 15

t was unbelievable that I would soon meet with Tim Sloan, that he would stand n front of me and that I would see what he looked like after all these years of hinking about him and his sister.

or all of my adult life I had thought of them. Countless times, I had wondered ow they survived their trauma, whether they resembled their mother, what ind of people they were and whether they hated me with their whole souls. I ad imagined unexpectedly crossing paths with them and having the conversa-on I so desperately wanted to have. In my imaginary meetings, I would grasp neir hands and embrace them tightly, then tell them I would turn back the ock if I could. I would vow to them to spend my life making amends for their other's death.

espite the wanderings of my mind, I never expected in reality to be planning a eeting with one of them. We had made contact with Tim and he knew about e. He had agreed to *meet* with me—not just accept a letter from me—knowing e role I had played in the course of his life. He had not declined to meet with e or declared that he never wanted to speak of me or cursed my name. It was fficult for me to grasp how casual his response to Reverend Williams had been nen I had imagined it being quite contrary.

assed the few days until my next therapy session replaying his words in my nd and wondering what he must have been thinking that day when he walked ay from his pastor.

turday came and it was finally time to sit down and talk to Dr. Young in per-n, for the two of us to dissect and digest what was happening before she ned Tim to arrange the meeting.

ared minor concerns about when and where we would meet and major con-ns, like how overwhelmed I was and whether, after having more time to think ough his feelings, Tim would change his mind about meeting with me. After he had had no warning before Reverend Williams approached him with a question that no doubt catapulted his past into his present. Would he tell his father or sister that I had approached him? Would they dissuade him from seeing me, or encourage him? Will he be angry with me? What will he say? What will I say?

"Are you sure this is what you want to do?" Dr. Young asked me. I could hear the worry in her voice.

I knew what could happen, but I also knew this was something I had longed for. There was no doubt in my mind about my answer.

"Yes."

"Okay. Then I'll call him and we'll work out the details," my blessed angel therapist said.

She asked me where I would be comfortable meeting with Tim and we talked at length about it. At first, I suggested meeting at a park near his father's house that I had seen during my many drive-bys. But it was nearing autumn; the weather was turning cold and rain was in the forecast. Then we discussed the idea of meeting in a public place like a coffeehouse, since I would be meeting with a complete stranger who may harbor ill will toward me. That also was not a good plan because of the subject matter of the meeting and my unstable emotional state. I wasn't sure if I could hold it together through our conversation and I didn't want anyone in public—or worse, someone I knew—to see me fall to pieces.

I told her I could meet him any time at all; I couldn't imagine anything that would stand in the way. We ended that morning with a plan to have Dr. Young call Tim about a date and time, the place to be determined later. When I left her office, all the nerve endings in my body were buzzing and I could feel my blood coursing through my veins. The anticipation of her next call to me began before I had even reached out my hand to open my car door.

　　　　★　　　　　　　★　　　　　　　★

My phone rang a few days later. I saw on caller ID that it was Dr. Young and my palms began to sweat as I put the phone to my ear.

"Connie, I talked to Tim," she said. I could not glean a hint of what she would say from the tone of her voice.

I wanted to hear his every word repeated back to me. I inhaled deeply. "And what did he say?"

"He sounds like a wonderful guy, and he seemed very concerned for you."

Tears welled up in my eyes as I listened.

"He said the accident wasn't your fault. He said it was in God's hands."

They spilled out onto my face, little rivulets running down my cheeks.

"Their family has always been concerned about you. Tim said that he and his dad had just discussed you a few weeks ago, before the Reverend talked to him. He feels badly about never having reached out to you."

My shoulders shook as I held in the sobs. We sat there in a short silence.

Then Dr. Young softly repeated Tim's words. "It wasn't your fault, Connie; it was in God's hands."

I had heard these words before and perhaps had said or thought them myself, but they were never so powerful or meant so much as hearing it from Pat Sloan's son.

"He's very anxious to meet with you, but has some unfortunate schedule con-flicts and a planned vacation. So we arranged a meeting for October fifth," she said. It was nearly a month away. "He said he would call me later about the rest of the details."

I swallowed a sob and thanked her, this wonderful, caring woman who had given me unconditional support and nurturing for the last two years, who had scraped me from death's door and somehow helped me stay afloat.

I hung up the phone and dragged myself to the wall calendar in my kitchen, flip-ping the page to the next month and staring at the box numbered "5" through blurry eyes, until the sounds of crying drew my cat from her hiding place. I let her crawl around my ankles and rub herself against me for several minutes before I dropped the September page back into place, scooped her up, and held her against my aching heart.

*   *   *

Weeks in my life never passed so slowly.

I spent them working with as much focus as I could muster and thinking about what the meeting with Tim had in store for me and us. From all indications, it seemed the meeting could be a good experience, but I still could not help worrying. I had survived so many years with a warped sense of self-esteem and low expectations created by my teenage mind that it seemed silly to believe everything would be okay.

There were so many unknowns. What would he say? How would I handle it? I was concerned that I was not entering into a meeting with Tim on solid emotional ground. Had this situation presented itself years before, when Jamie and I were together and I felt emotionally sound, it would have been completely different. I would have had the emotional support of someone who loved me, but now I was physically and emotionally alone and suffering from a disorder that creates a world without logic and overpowering emotions. To meet with Tim now, when I was finally confronting PTSD and struggling to recreate meaning and trust in a positive way—while still being dramatically consumed by this event from my past—seemed an invitation for emotional disaster. I was about to face a very tender and personal part of my past and I was petrified.

Dr. Young had the same concerns. She was very worried about me meeting Tim alone and offered several times to facilitate the meeting, knowing the extent of my emotional vulnerability. I declined all her offers, perhaps against my better judgment. Meeting Tim was something I wanted to do on my own.

With one week left before the meeting, Tim called Dr. Young and they discussed the details. I had told her that I felt I should go to him, the least I could do for him. But after the park and coffeehouse ideas fizzled, the only other alternatives were meeting at Dr. Young's office, at either Tim's or my church, or at one of our houses. Dr. Young reported that Tim had graciously offered to meet at my house, and that he would be there at three o'clock the following Sunday.

For so many years, he had seemed almost unreal to me, the fictional name of a character in a story, and now he was coming to my house. Tim Sloan, surviving son of Pat, a real person who I had never met but with whom I had a personal connection, would stand at my doorstep just days from now.

What would he look like? Would he look like his mother? What would he say? What, in God's name, would I say to him?

*   *   *

The last week crept by as time does when you're only thinking of one thing.

When Saturday came, I met with Dr. Young, our last session before I saw Tim. She was still concerned about me going it alone and again offered to be there.

"You need support and I really wish you would let me help. I'm sure Tim won't mind if we call today and change the location to my office," she said.

I knew she was right—I did need her. But I had withdrawn so much in the past few months from all my family and friends that I was used to a solitary existence and didn't want to ask anyone to accompany me. On some level, I think I had come to trust only myself throughout my life, and thought I was capable of handling the big stuff alone. As Dr. Young taught me, it takes a long time to reestablish faith and trust in people after trauma, especially when people failed you after your experience. When I had needed people the most in my life, I had been disappointed. Perhaps that made me unable to see the choice to trust when it was there in front of me.

Despite that Dr. Young had always been there for me, my instincts, however poor, told me I should go through the meeting on my own.

"Thank you, but I think I'll be okay," I answered, avoiding her gaze.

"Darn it, Connie! Why do you have to try to take on all this alone? Why won't you reach out?" She was angry and frustrated with me, and rightly so.

I had no answer for her questions so we sat in silence for a moment, me looking at the floor and her looking up and out the window as if to ask God what it would take to get through to me.

After a moment, she looked back at me and said, "Okay. I will be here before, during, and after your meeting if you need me. All you have to do is call."

I knew at the very least that I needed her support after the visit. I was certa
that I needed to be able to pick up the phone, dial her number and hear h
comforting voice over the line. I felt terrible for the worry I would cause her ov
the next thirty-two hours, but also reassured that another soul knew what I w
about to do, understood the magnitude of it, and would wait for my call.

Dr. Young stood at the end of our time and offered her help once again, stres
ing that she would be available at any time on Sunday. We hugged and s
wished me luck. As I turned and left her office, my haven for the last two yea
I felt as if I had climbed onto the highest branch of a soaring tree and fac
scaling the last ten feet with no foothold.

The next day and a half would be excruciatingly long. I got in my car and dro
to the cemetery. With this visit, I wanted to tell Pat that I would be meeti
with her son.

As I drove, I prayed again that I was doing the right thing.

    *   *   *

That night, I reread the letter I had written but never sent to Tim and Bonnie
made some slight changes, but nothing that detracted from the message. It w
the only answer I could find to the "What will I say?" questions that we
swirling through my mind, the best tool I felt I had to convey my sympathy.

I thought, *if I totally break down I can just hand it to him. It would still be r
talking, even if I'm not really talking.*

After a long evening of restlessness and mounting fears, and exhausted from r
thoughts and worries, I turned in early to bed. Even as I fell asleep, I could n
shake the fog of disbelief enveloping me. The boy in my mind had become a m
who was willing to see me. If the lost girl I was long ago had had any idea th
would happen, she might have lived a life filled with hope and not despair.

    *   *   *

Sunday morning, October 5, 2003, I woke early and went to church. I pray
that this day would bring peace and comfort to Tim and me. I sat next to r
family, them not knowing anything about what was going on in my life, abo
to do the most important and meaningful thing I had ever done.

After church, with Tim's arrival still five hours away and my empty house making me restless and anxious, I went to the grocery store to pass some time and try to calm my nerves. As I strolled aimlessly through the aisles with an empty shopping cart, looking at shelves of products I didn't need, it briefly crossed my mind that I had invited someone I did not know to my house to be alone with me. A complete stranger, whom I had never met and could not pick out in a crowd, who may have a heart filled with dangerous anger for me, would soon knock on my door and enter my private world.

Logically, I knew it was unwise to do it alone. But I did not flinch at the thought; I just didn't care what harm might befall me. I knew without a doubt that it was what I wanted.

After an hour or so, I drove home again and tried to immerse myself in my usual Sunday afternoon pursuits to curb my anxiety. I fumbled with the remote control and tuned into the day's televised football games. Most Sundays I watched all the games and constantly scanned the scores. I usually listened intently to the announcers calling the games and mentally critiqued their critiques. This time, I couldn't focus on the screen, and though I stared at it for a few hours and flipped constantly between channels, I wouldn't have been able to say who was playing or won. The announcers' voices droned on until their words melted into chaotic, spinning noise in my head.

My pulse raced but the clock's hands did not. Finally, there were twenty minutes until Tim's arrival. I thought of how it would begin, perhaps with me opening the door and saying, "Hi Tim, I'm Connie," and reaching out my hand for a welcoming handshake. I wondered about him for the billionth time. Then there were twelve minutes left. I picked up a pen and tried to write in my journal about how I felt at that moment, but only managed a few words before the doorbell rang.

I rubbed my damp palms together and had the conflicting thoughts *I can't believe it's finally time!* and *Is it time already?*

I stood up, breathed deeply and walked toward the door.

*   *   *

When I opened it, I stood face to face with a man who appeared friendly and gentle, with a pleasant expression on his face.

"Are you Connie?" he asked.

I said yes, and he quickly followed with, "Hi, I'm Tim Sloan."

I reached out my hand to him, hoping he would accept it. "Hi, Tim. Thank you for coming."

He stepped toward me and instead of shaking my hand, opened his arms and wrapped me in a warm embrace. I nearly crumbled.

Holding back my emotions, I invited him in and he obliged. As we walked to the kitchen, he asked, "So, how are you?"

I thought to myself, *How do I begin to answer that? That alone could take hours.*

Smiling at him, I replied, "I'm doing okay."

"And your mother?" he asked.

"She's very well, thank you."

I motioned to the kitchen table and we sat down. Tim continued, "Dad told me that she came to the funeral home."

"Yes, she did." I thought to myself that my mother's gesture must have been appreciated by his father, and wondered as I had so many times in the past, how different things might have been if I, too, had gone.

The ice broken, we opened up and talked, sitting across from each other at my kitchen table over cups of coffee, for over two hours. After twenty-five years of silence, I looked in his eyes and told him how deeply sorry I was for my involvement in his mother's death, and that he and his sister had always lived in my thoughts and prayers. When the words were in the air between us and he finally knew, I felt that if I did nothing else in my life it would not matter. He knew.

Tim shared memories of his mother and the day she died.

"I was called to the office and saw my dad waiting for me. I wondered as I went to him why he was there. He told me that Mom had been in a car accident, and I knew, without him telling me, that she had died."

I thought of what it had been like for me to try to understand death as an eight-year-old child, to comprehend that it had claimed my father—that I would never see him again. Tim had gone through it, too.

He went on talking about that day but then stopped abruptly, recognizing what both Dr. Young and I had noticed a few months earlier.

He looked at me intensely and said, "Wow, you look so much like my mom! I can't believe how much you look like Mom. Have you seen a picture of her? You really look alike."

"Yes, I found a picture of her and I was pretty surprised at the resemblance, too," I answered.

He continued, amazed. "I think you and Dad should meet, but I'm glad he didn't come with me today. At least now I can warn him how much you look like her."

Tim shared much about himself and his family that day. Some stories brought me comfort; I learned that his father and stepmother had been married twenty years and Tim and his wife had two children they adored. Other stories were difficult to hear, and the sorrow I felt surged forth in fresh waves.

He said again that he believed the day of the crash was in God's hands.

"It was Mom's time to go, but it wasn't yours," he said. I could hardly believe he did not resent me. I don't know what I would have believed had the tables been turned.

I told him I visited the cemetery on occasion and asked him who tended the flowers at his mother's grave.

He raised his eyebrows in surprise, "You go to the cemetery?" he asked. He continued, "I don't go very often, maybe a couple times a year. But I'm not sure why I go. She isn't there. At least I don't think she's there." He paused. "But she's here right now. She is definitely here with us right now."

"Yes, I know," I said with a weak smile, struggling not to cry.

Realizing that I could not speak just then, Tim went on to say he had told his father about the phone call from Dr. Young; that he had known immediately he wanted to meet me and wanted his father to as well.

"I thought it was better I come first, alone, because I wasn't sure what to expect and was worried about Dad meeting you before I had the chance to see if everything would be okay."

I nodded my agreement, and hoped that his father was serious about wanting to meet with me.

With a look of concern on his face, Tim continued, "Bonnie doesn't know about any of this yet."

I looked at him, wondering. "Will she be upset?" I asked.

"I think it's going to take some time for her to understand why I came here," he replied. Tim shared many things with me that day about Bonnie, but I could tell he was hesitant about divulging too much. I wondered about her perception of the crash and me, but did not press the matter.

"I understand. I can't tell you what it means to me that you came here today."

As our conversation ended, we exchanged phone numbers. Then I walked him to the door.

Tim turned to face me on the doorstep. "I'd like to keep in touch with you, Connie," he said. Though I had said little about my life and nothing about my struggle with PTSD, he seemed very concerned about my emotional well-being. He said several times that he hoped I would take good care of myself in the future.

"I'd like that too," I said. I gave Pat's caring, considerate son a warm hug and we said goodbye.

I walked back into my house and sat there in silence for several long minutes, absorbing it. Finally, I had met Tim Sloan. I knew what he looked like and had learned about his life. And he knew, after all these years, that I did not just walk away from the accident without a thought. I was happy to have met him and been in his presence.

Some of my questions had been answered, and I was glad of that. I felt comforted by Tim's faith that the accident was in God's hands and that it happened for reasons unknown to us. I was relieved to know that neither he nor his father resented or blamed me for Pat's death, and that they had both moved on and found happiness.

The visit helped open my eyes to see some things in a different, real way, not through the lens of the negative belief system that had taken over my life.

I knew Dr. Young was waiting for my call; my phone had rung two times during the visit. After sitting in silence for some time replaying the three hours with him, I picked up the phone to tell her about it.

Chapter 16

The rest of the evening was hazy.

It was hard to believe that I had just seen Tim and miraculously, he did not hate me. When I turned in to bed later, I pictured his kind face and heard his heartfelt words again in my mind. I slept soundly.

The following day I left for a business trip to California.

When Dr. Young had set up the meeting between Tim and me, I was extremely anxious about how things would go and how I would feel afterward. A long ride on an airplane the day after seemed a better option than trying to keep my emotions in check at my office. Having the freedom to make my own travel schedule was a blessing. The only thing I intended to do that day was fly and think; I had planned no meetings or appointments so I could be alone and far away from my daily life.

When I arrived, I checked in to my hotel and spent the afternoon reflecting on all that had happened over the two years that led me to Tim. I replayed our conversation repeatedly in my mind and wondered if, in the future, I would be fortunate enough to share similar time with Tim's father—something Tim had encouraged—and with Bonnie.

Tim had not even mentioned the potential for a meeting between Bonnie and me, and had been concerned about her even knowing that we had made contact through Reverend Williams. Would Tim tell her we had met? What would she think? Her feelings about the crash and the loss of her mother, though surely complex and painful, were unclear to me. Although Tim had shared many things about Bonnie, he did not share much about that.

Having met with Tim, I felt a sense of urgency about sharing my sorrow with Bonnie. I wanted to meet with her as soon as I could but it was not within my control. I knew she might be reticent about meeting me, and that things had to happen in their own time (if they were to happen at all). I could not push it.

trusted that Tim would know best what to do and was prepared for a long wait until the right opportunity arrived.

didn't realize how soon it would come.

That evening, just over twenty-four hours after Tim had left my home, my cell phone rang as I walked leisurely near my hotel. I answered it thinking it was a work-related call.

t was not.

"Hi, is this Connie?" a female voice asked.

"Yes, it is," I replied, not recognizing it.

Then she said, "This is Bonnie, Tim's sister."

stopped walking and stood there, my well-rehearsed, imagined words to her escaping me. My voice, and the beating of my heart, nearly failed me.

stuttered a greeting and she quickly said, "Tim said I should give you a call."

So he *had* told her about our meeting. Almost immediately. I was glad of that, but I was concerned because she sounded awkward and tense (as I surely did). I didn't know what she wanted me to say, or what Tim's account of our meeting had implied I would say. I had so many things to say to her, but she had caught me unsuspecting and all I could say was, "Okay..." like some crazy fool.

There was silence for a long moment.

Then she asked, "So, did you talk to her?"

At first, I had no idea who "her" was. It took me a moment to check my emotions and calm my mind before I understood the question. Then I swallowed a fisted lump.

"You mean, did I talk to your mom?" I asked.

"Yes," she answered. "Did you talk to her?"

Oh my God, this is not happening, I thought. Bonnie had asked me a question she had probably wanted an answer to for her whole life. And I had to answer it while standing alone on a road I didn't know, three thousand miles from home, talking on a cell phone to a grown woman who still had a grieving five-year-old child inside her.

"No," I began, trembling though the weather was balmy. "We were...our cars were across the road from each other. I tried to get out and go to her but I kept falling down. Someone helped me back to the car."

"Do you know anyone who was there?"

I thought of my brother Rick, a volunteer firefighter at the scene of the crash. He might be able to tell Bonnie if her mother had said anything before she died. But how could I ever ask him? We had never discussed anything about that day or my life after it; doing it now would be terrifying. None of my family knew what I had been through and envisioning scenarios about telling them made my palms sweat and my pulse quicken.

In spite of it, I said softly, "I might know someone who could help." Just saying the words made me panicky, fearful of what my offer meant.

Bonnie said, her voice crackling across the distant signal, "The story I heard was that she died in the ambulance on the way to the hospital."

Oh, God, why is this happening this way?

I struggled to keep from crying into the phone and told her gently that I did not think that was true. Biting my lip and trying to focus, I said, "I'm not sure, Bonnie, but I believe she may have died at the scene."

She quickly moved on. "I didn't know until a year ago that it was a head-on collision. I had heard she was run off the road by someone trying to pass her."

Although I had not been encouraged to talk about the accident and people around me never spoke of it, I couldn't believe this woman was not told the details of her mother's death until she was over thirty years old.

"But you know now that isn't true, don't you?" I asked.

"Yes."

As the strained conversation continued it became scattered, Bonnie talking first about the crash and then about her mother and her own life. Her pain was palpable; I could hear in her voice that she had had a very different journey to that point than her brother and that she, like me, had not received much support along the way. As she spoke, I felt sympathy and sorrow and completely helpless. I wanted to snap my fingers and dissolve her pain.

The conversation stalled after several minutes but I didn't want that to be the end. I wanted to tell her so, but I also didn't want to cause her further discomfort.

I said, "I want you to know that you and Tim have always been in my thoughts. If you ever want to talk about anything, I would be happy to listen."

"Well, I wouldn't mind, but I don't think it will help you much," she said. "I don't think I can say much that you would want to hear."

I looked up at the sky and listened to myriad possible word combinations flying through my mind, finding none that satisfied me. All I could manage was, "That's okay. Look, the last thing I want to do is stir up things for you. That's why I never tried to contact you in the past. But I have always wanted you to know how terribly sorry I am that this happened, and hoped you were doing as well as possible."

Bonnie answered, "I'm not doing well, but you can't fill the void."

"I know I can't," I said. I paused and then asked, "Do you talk to anyone about this?"

No, not really. I started to talk to my pastor about it recently but he hasn't been much help. I even mentioned you and he said that you had probably moved on by now."

"No," I answered in a raspy voice.

There was another awkward silence, neither of us knowing what to say or how to end the conversation. I was utterly without words to ease her suffering.

Then she told me she had a sixteen-month-old daughter named Alesha.

"One positive thing is that if Mom had lived I probably wouldn't be here with her," Bonnie said. "I wouldn't trade her for the world!" Then after a moment she continued, "Things would be different." She didn't elaborate on what that meant and I did not ask. Instead, I asked her some questions about Alesha to bring some light into the dark conversation.

We spoke a few more seconds before Bonnie quickly stopped and apologized in advance for her depleted cell phone battery and our certain disconnection.

I told her again, "You always have been and will be in my thoughts. Please call me if you ever want to talk." I told her she would be in my prayers and we said goodbye.

I stood outside my hotel and sobbed as the enormity of meeting each of Pat's children in the span of one day set in. I was still trying to process the meeting with Tim, and *that* one had been planned. The unplanned phone meeting with Bonnie was a hole in the boat of my emotions; the little water that had kept me afloat was rushing out and I felt myself sinking fast.

I cried because I had wanted to cry when Tim offered me a hug in lieu of his hand; and when he sat at my kitchen table for three hours and told me that the accident wasn't my fault; and when I stuffed my travel bag under my seat and felt the plane ascend into the clouds. I cried because I couldn't help Bonnie when she so badly needed someone; and because my ability to remain stalwart when I wanted to lay on the floor in the fetal position was gone.

Eventually, I dragged myself to my hotel room, left Dr. Young a phone message and crawled into bed, curling into a tight ball and pulling the covers up over my ears so I could try not to hear myself think.

*   *   *

I woke early the next morning after a restless night. I had not been awake long when my cell phone rang.

It was Bonnie.

"Who is this?" she asked.

"This is Connie Bachman," I said, once again caught utterly off guard.

"Oh my gosh, I must have called you by mistake. I'm so sorry," she said, sounding flustered and embarrassed. She briefly explained the error and seemed much less tense than the night before.

Since I had been very concerned for her after our first conversation, I asked how she felt, acknowledging how difficult it must be for her to be in touch with me. She told me she felt alright and quickly admitted that our previous conversation had been awkward. I agreed.

With that we fell into an easier conversation and talked for a few minutes. I closed once again with my offer to be there if she needed to talk and she extended the same offer. Then she gave me her e-mail address, saying it would be easier to reach her that way.

My heart did cartwheels. I was grateful that she called, albeit by mistake, and felt slightly better about our contact. I saw her e-mail address as a positive sign and was hopeful that that medium would be a way for us to continue communicating. I wanted so much to speak with her again; I wanted so much to help her though I was not sure if or how I could.

For the rest of the day I struggled to focus on my work but was consumed with thoughts of Bonnie and what growing up without her mother must have been like. From our brief conversations I had learned that she was angry about the void in her life, and that she blamed it and lack of guidance for some of her wrong life choices. I could not imagine what life had been like for her.

All day I asked myself, why did Bonnie call me at all? Was it because Tim asked her to call in hopes that it would help *me*, or was it because she had hoped to find some answers to things she had always wondered? I'm sure it was a bit of both, and when the day and my musings ended, I realized I really didn't need to know why she had called. It was enough that she had called.

*   *   *

My stay in California was brief and I was soon back in Columbus and behind my office desk. Bonnie had given me her contact information and I intended to use it; I had thought of what I would write to her almost the entire flight home.

I had run the following idea by Dr. Young when I had spoken to her from California: would she be open to meeting with Bonnie? I wanted to offer Bonnie *something*; maybe a conversation with someone who cared about people as much as Dr. Young did would help her start her own journey toward healing.

Dr. Young told me she would check with her peers due to the uniqueness of the situation, and conditionally agreed to do it.

With that in mind, I sent an email to Bonnie. I thanked her for calling and hoped she was doing okay. As I had before, I offered for her to meet with me but this time also offered a possible meeting with Dr. Young. I explained what a wonderful and caring person she is and that she may be able to help us both with the situation. I again expressed my concern for her and the situation.

As I sent it I had the conflicting thoughts *Why did I send that?* and *I hope she responds.* Of course, there was a very real possibility that she would not reply, that it was too painful for her to be in touch with me and I was not the person to give her comfort and compassion. Perhaps she had asked all of her questions and, finding that I knew nothing more about her mother than I told her, would decide to move elsewhere in her search for answers.

But what if she *did* respond? What would she say? Would she tell me to shove off and leave her alone to deal with her past without my meddling? Would she be bitter at my stirring up painful memories for her? Was this all a mistake? Or would she take me up on my offer and say, "I want to meet you face to face Connie. I need to see you and talk to you in person?"

I didn't have to wait long for my answers; I soon received a reply.

At first I was puzzled when I noticed that the subject of the message said, "FW: (indicating that she was forwarding to me a message sent to her): A Butterfly Lesson." We certainly had not established enough of a rapport to forward each other e-mail messages containing words of wisdom, jokes and the like, but I was elated to see a response at all and quickly opened the mail.

found a note from Bonnie saying that she had received the following message the day she first called me:

"A Butterfly's Lesson"

One day, a small opening appeared in a cocoon. A man sat and watched the butterfly for several hours as it struggled to force its body through that little hole.

Soon, it seemed to stop making progress. It appeared to the man as if it had gotten as far as it could and could go no further. So the man decided to help the butterfly; he took a pair of scissors and opened the cocoon.
The butterfly then emerged easily. But it had a withered body; it was tiny and had shriveled wings. The man continued to watch because he expected that, at any moment, the wings would open, enlarge and expand to be able to support the butterfly's body, and become firm.

Neither happened! In fact, the butterfly spent the rest of its life crawling around with a withered body and shriveled wings. It never was able to fly.

What the man in his kindness and his goodwill did not understand was that the restricting cocoon and the struggle required for the butterfly to get through the tiny opening were God's way of forcing fluid from the body of the butterfly into its wings, so that it would be ready for flight once it achieved its freedom from the cocoon.

Sometimes, struggles are exactly what we need in our life.
If God allowed us to go through our life without any obstacles, it would cripple us. We would not be as strong as we could have been, never be able to fly.

nished reading it, put my head in my hands, and cried. It was powerful and ke volumes about the lives of Bonnie, Tim and I. I thanked God for His inter-tion and felt—for the first time—that contact with Bonnie was for the best that she would see that, too. I stayed like that for some time, just crying and king to God at my desk with the door closed, asking Him for guidance.

*   *   *

Within minutes, I received another message from Bonnie. In it, she revealed a bit about what it had been like for her to lose her mother so young, and find, as she grew up, that few people understood or empathized with her pain.

As I read her words, I thought of how many years I had felt the same way—that people had abandoned me when I needed them most; that I was abnormal; that whatever it was I suffered from I needed to "get over" so I could "fit in" with functional society. Both Bonnie and I knew it is not so simple. There is so much more to dealing with personal traumas than just dusting off your clothes after your life explodes. Wounds need to be cleaned and dressed and mended, and edifices need to be rebuilt before life can move forward again. And those things cannot be accomplished in a solitary effort.

Her message also said that she wanted to meet with me. I was elated; I wanted badly to see and maybe help her, but I was concerned about how much I should involve myself in her life. After all, I was not in a healthy emotional place either and hearing more about her story would doubtless be painful for me. At a minimum, I wanted to respond to her telling, emotional message as soon as possible.

I responded to Bonnie almost immediately letting her know how pleased I was that she wanted to meet with me. I thanked her for sharing some of what she had been through since her mother died and also explained how much I understood and could relate to some of her frustrations through coping with my own struggles.

*   *   *

Although I had offered to meet with Bonnie and I knew it was something I really wanted to do, I was not sure I could do it alone. Dr. Young had tried to talk me out of meeting with Tim unaided; I had adhered stubbornly to the idea that I could handle it and had convinced her of that. Now, though, I knew I needed her to faciliate a meeting between me and Bonnie. Bonnie's experience with the loss of her mother had been markedly different than Tim's. If we were going to talk more about that in a face-to-face meeting when my emotional state was hanging in the balance, I would need support.

I called Dr. Young to ask her for it.

"I know you said you would meet with Bonnie if she wanted to arrange a session with you," I began. "And I don't know if she would want me there."

"Yes, I will," she replied.

I continued, "But she wants to see *me*, and I need *you* there."

"It's about time you asked," she said.

         *   *   *

Bonnie contacted me again and I was relieved to hear that she was not opposed to Dr. Young's presence at a meeting between us. We scheduled a time and place to meet and then, once again I sat and waited, wondering what would happen and whether I would be able to handle it.

I prayed that it was the right thing to do for all of us, and that maybe in time Bonnie and I both would feel peace in our tormented hearts.

Chapter 17

The meeting with Bonnie would be just ten days after I had met her brother.

Never, in all my contemplation of them, did I consider the possibility of meeting them face to face. That it was happening was a near miracle, and, not accustomed to miracles, it was like trying to digest a feast for a thousand when all I had room for was a spot of tea.

Then there was the timing: my visit with Tim had still been new and unprocessed when the call came from Bonnie and the wheels were set in motion for our introduction.

As the interim days passed, I recalled the adage, "Be careful what you wish for." I had always hoped at least to know them; at most, to make amends. But I got what I had wanted while swimming in the sea of a raging mental disorder, and managing it all at once was possibly more than I could handle.

Bonnie and I were to meet on a Wednesday evening after work at Dr. Young's office.

I was grateful that she had agreed to mediate. My anxiety was different than it had been before meeting Tim; the feelings he had shared with her about the crash had made me feel safe. If that had not been so, I doubt I would have been willing or able to meet him without her there.

With Bonnie, it was different.

I could tell from our phone conversations and e-mails that her mother's death was still fresh. Her feelings toward me were unsettled at a minimum; I could see that she appreciated that I cared enough to make an appearance in her life, but she had also believed for most of her life that I had run her mother off the road and then driven away into my life. She had grown into a woman without maternal care, a denser path filled with sharper brambles for a daughter than a son. was terrified that meeting Bonnie, and potentially being the target of her unreleased anguish, could trigger an emotional tsunami that had been brewing for years and would sweep me away.

The day of our meeting soon arrived and I contacted Bonnie to confirm it and give her directions to Dr. Young's office in Columbus from her workplace near Marysville, forty-five minutes away. Her reply offered up something I did not expect: a pre-meeting dinner invitation. In the second it took to decide I would accept, my terror skyrocketed. I had mentally prepared myself to meet her in the presence of a third party who would provide me with security in my perilous emotional state. But I had waited so long to see her that I could not consider declining, even though I would do it alone and at extreme emotional risk.

*   *   *

The restaurant was just a few blocks from Dr. Young's office, chosen partly because I knew I could dash there quickly in the event of an emergency.

I arrived early and nervous. I took a seat in the waiting area and watched closely at length every person who walked in the door. I tapped my feet and imagined what Bonnie would look like, what we would say. I fiddled with the book on my lap I had brought for her. Entitled *Motherless Daughters*, I knew from a friend that the book's author, Hope Edelman, had brought comfort to many grieving women through shared stories of loss. I hoped it would bring Bonnie some of the same comfort. I hoped it would be appropriate, and show I cared.

Soon, amidst all the couples approaching the door walked a woman, alone. I watched through the window as she closed her car door and turned toward me. I had pictured what Bonnie might look like in her early thirties, perhaps with dark blond hair and a fresh, gentle face, like her mother. I thought to myself, my pulse quickening, *That can't be her.* She was not at all like my mind's picture; it didn't *feel* like she was Bonnie. The woman walked directly to the door and promptly through it into the restaurant, passing me without a glance. My heart settled a bit, and I took a deep, cleansing breath before I looked out the window again.

I did, another single woman was reaching for the door handle. She was on the other side of the glass not five feet from me; I knew it was Bonnie in an instant. I stood as she entered the door and stepped toward her.

As soon as we made eye contact, I asked, nervously, "Are you Bonnie?"

"Yes," she said kindly. "Hello, Connie."

We shook hands and I hoped she could not feel the sweat in my palms.

"Thanks so much for driving all the way here, and for meeting me," I said.

Bonnie smiled briefly in response and then let herself be led to our table. I followed behind, wondering how in the world I was supposed to sit across the table from her and eat.

As we settled into our seats, she looked at me intently and said, "It's true what Tim said. You look so much like my mother. I'm glad he told me before I saw you."

I didn't know how to reply, so I paused a moment and looked down at my hands. Then I said what I had always wanted to say.

"I want you to know how very sorry I am for what happened, Bonnie. I'm sorry that you lost your mom and that I had something to do with that. I've wished all my life that I could change it."

There! I had said it. Both Tim and Bonnie knew now. Under the table, I wiped my palms on my pants and held one hand safely in the other.

"Thank you," she said. "I appreciate that you've thought of her and us."

From there, the conversation flowed. We spoke no more of the crash; she asked for no details. Instead, she told me of her childhood, growing up with her brother and father and her father's remarriage. She spoke of her husband and Alesha. When she talked about her little girl, her eyes lit up and she beamed with pride. I knew in my heart that she had committed herself to being the best mother she could be and I knew why she had made the commitment. I gave her the book I had brought for her. I think she was happy that I—that someone made an effort to comfort her and recognize her pain.

She mentioned, again, how much I resembled her mother.

"I brought some pictures of her with me," Bonnie said. "We only have a few. I have them with me. Would you like to see them?"

Remembering what happened when I had found Pat's high school yearbook pho-tograph, I was unsure I should see them in the middle of a restaurant. But I longed to see them and did not decline. I took a discreet deep breath and accepted the picture she offered; saw Pat's face so much like my own. I could only hold my eyes on it long enough for Bonnie to describe its setting. Then, I politely returned it and made work of settling the bill to force back the tears.

"I have a few others in the car," Bonnie said. "I'll bring them in with me to our appointment."

Please don't, I could have said. *Please, don't.*

But I *needed* to see them.

"That would be nice," I said.

*   *   *

When we arrived, Dr. Young was still with a patient, so we had to sit in the wait-ing area for a few moments. As soon as we did, Bonnie reached into her purse and brought out two more photographs of her mother. She handed one to me.

"This one is of her in her horse barn," she said with a smile. "She loved horses. I don't think she would ever have lived anywhere but on that farm. Pepper was her favorite. She adored that horse."

She paused.

"I guess that's why I have a horse farm, too," she said quietly. Then, louder, "Alesha just squeals with laughter when she gets to ride."

I could not say a word. I just sat there with a small smile plastered on my face, my teeth clenched inside my mouth.

Then, Bonnie pulled out the last picture. It was of Pat, standing on a ladder and hanging a Christmas ornament on the wall.

"I was told this picture was taken the night before the accident."

To say I did not expect to hear that would be a monumental understatement. As I looked down at it, my head flooded with thoughts of what it must have been like for Bonnie and her brother to face Christmas nine days after losing their mother, and every Christmas afterward. I thought of my own mother, how she had been there each Christmas and every day of my life. I thought of what Pat might have been thinking as her husband snapped her picture: *I hope the kids have fun this year; I have to pick up the doll Bonnie wants so badly; Tim will be upset if he doesn't get that dump truck; I'll take them to see Santa on Saturday.* How could she know what the next day held for her?

I was grateful that, just then, Dr. Young opened the door to her office. Unwittingly, she saved me again.

*   *   *

She approached us with a smile and extended her hand to Bonnie in introduction. Bonnie put the picture in her purse and stood to greet her.

"I'm Samantha Young," she said warmly, shaking Bonnie's hand with both of her own. "I'm happy you're here."

Then she looked over at me and smiled a proud parent's smile, as if to say, "Here you are, after all this time and hard work, walking into my office with Bonnie Sloan." Instead, she said, "It's good to see you, Connie."

"Thanks," I managed with a small smile, a lump forming in my throat. "You, too."

Dr. Young led us into her office and invited us to make ourselves comfortable. I waited, nervous for what might happen during the one hour she had set aside for us, while Bonnie chose a seat. I knew that Dr. Young had no planned agenda and intended to let the conversation flow based on Bonnie's cues. There was no other person in the world I would rather have been at the helm at that moment than my therapist. I trusted that her nurturing manner and intuitive skills would make Bonnie feel comfortable and understood.

After we sat, Dr. Young looked at Bonnie with caring in her eyes and said, "It must have come as quite a shock to you when your brother told you that he had met Connie."

Bonnie hesitated briefly, as if remembering the moment.

"Yes, it did," she said, her hands clasped together in her lap. "It took awhile to sink in."

From that point on, the conversation included only Bonnie and Dr. Young.

I sat in almost complete silence and listened as Bonnie told the story of a painful life. She didn't focus on the accident, or my role in it, at all. Like me, Bonnie had bottled up years of hurt and had had no one to turn to for support, no one to help her process her pain in a healthy way. Finally having found a caring person to listen, she told Dr. Young everything she had wanted *anyone* to listen to for most of her life. I wrung my hands and stared at my lap and inhaled deeply to stifle sorrowful moans as I heard her tell of how growing up without her mother had affected her life choices and caused her to feel great regret about many of them.

I had discovered in our brief communications that Bonnie is a strong, independent woman—qualities I knew from my conversation with Tim that she inherited from her mother. Even so, it must have been difficult for her to share that kind of raw emotion with us. As I listened, I just wanted to work magic and make it all go away. Negative thoughts ran through my mind, like, *If I wouldn't have been there that day she would have been spared all this*; and, *I don't deserve to be happy when her childhood was taken from her.* As the minutes ticked by and our allotted hour neared two, it was nearly unbearable to listen.

Dr. Young knew it. She needed to stay in the moment with Bonnie as Bonnie spoke and cried, but she took her eyes off her whenever it was possible to glance at me. Her brief eye contact spoke volumes: *I'm listening to her, and I'm also worried about you.* A few times, when my own glances failed to convey my unspoken assurance that I was okay, Dr. Young stopped and asked, her tone filled with concern, "Connie, are you alright? I know this has to be tough for you."

I nodded slowly. "I'm fine. Really. Please go ahead."

I clenched my teeth as the distraught woman in my head cackled maniacally at the absurdity of my words.

*   *   *

Dr. Young finally chose an appropriate moment to bring the session with Bonnie and me to a close. It was difficult, but necessary. We were spent.

With her help, I again offered Bonnie my deepest sympathies.

"Please know that I care, and I've always cared," I said, my throat tight. "I've thought about you and your mom and your brother, your whole family, for so long..."

I had to stop then. With a worried glance at me, Dr. Young stepped in quickly and offered Bonnie some guidance on where to turn, closer to home, if she wanted to talk more about the things she had shared with us. Bonnie thanked her, and we left Dr. Young's office together.

As we reached the parking lot, I stopped and turned to her. She held out her arms to me, and I took them. We stood in a warm embrace for a moment and I struggled for the right words.

How do you properly thank a person for something like what Bonnie did for me? How do you tell them you're grateful that they agreed to meet you when your very existence caused them so much sadness and pain? There are no words; there weren't then and there aren't now.

We pulled apart and I said to her, "Thank you. Thank you for meeting me, and for everything. I hope you're doing okay."

Her eyes were red from the long, emotional session. "Knowing you care means a lot to me," she replied. "Knowing just might help me find some closure to all this."

She opened the door to her car. "I'm fine. I'll be fine." She smiled at me. "Thanks for dinner, and for the book, too."

I smiled and raised my hand in a small wave as she backed out her car and drove away.

*　　　　　*　　　　　*

I stepped into my car and laid my head back on the seat, then closed my eyes and exhaled a long breath that had been stuck in my lungs for two hours. I put my hand over my heart and pressed hard to try to quell the hurt. It felt raw, as if it had been torn from my chest and beaten. I wondered how it continued to beat.

After a few moments, I opened my eyes and tried to focus my efforts on the small task of turning the key in the ignition. I didn't notice Dr. Young leave the building; she just appeared at my car window.

I rolled it down.

With worry clouding her face, she asked, "Are you okay?"

"Yeah," I answered, my eyelids heavy and wanting to close. "At least I think so. I'm sorry we took so long."

"Don't worry about that. I felt so bad for you during the session and wish I could have helped you more. Are you sure you're okay?"

"I'm sort of overwhelmed, but I think I'll be fine," I lied. "I know you had to help her." I paused for a moment, looking at her. "I really appreciate everything you've done for me."

"I know," she replied, her look of concern still present. "I just wanted to know you're alright before you drive home. I want you to call me before Saturday if you need anything. Anything at all."

"I will." I offered a weak smile. "Thank you, Sam."

I watched her watch me drive away. When she could no longer see me, I let loose. I don't remember the drive home. I just remember crying the whole way; then when I let myself in the door to my house; then as I walked up the staircase to bed; then as I pulled up the covers.

Chapter 18

I never thought that saying "I'm sorry" would be a miracle drug. I didn't expect that it would magically erase years of survivor guilt, or cure post-traumatic stress disorder, or make me want to be with people again.

But I also did not expect, after meeting Tim and Bonnie, an onslaught of new painful feelings I did not understand. And I did not imagine that I would withdraw even further from my family and friends as I tried to sort through them.

The human heart can only take so much despair before it either sinks, or heaves overboard its unnecessary cargo and sails on.

*   *   *

The Saturday after the meeting with Bonnie I was back at Dr. Young's office, sitting in the seat Bonnie had sat in just a few days earlier. The words she had spoken over those two hours came flooding back to me in detail. She may as well have still been sitting in the room.

She may as well have been sitting on my back. I was dead weight; my body felt like wax in a mold, cooled and congealed and waiting to be scraped out. I had no idea where to go from there.

Dr. Young took things one careful step at a time.

"Have you talked to Bonnie since our meeting?" she asked, keeping me focused on details for a few minutes before delving into the tough stuff.

"Just by e-mail," I replied slowly. "I sent her a note from my office. I asked her she was alright and thanked her for coming so far to meet me."

"Did she respond?"

"Yes. She wrote back. She said it was hard to come here. But she seemed to be doing okay."

"It was pretty courageous of her," Dr. Young said, admiration in her voice. "I hope she uses the names I gave her to find someone nearby to talk to."

"Me, too."

She paused briefly, and I could see that she was ready to move on to me.

"My guess is that your caring about her will be a big first step for her in getting to a better place with all she's been through."

I could feel the emotion begin to swirl in my leaden chest. "I hope so," I replied, my voice trembling.

"But do you believe it will?" she asked gently.

I began to cry. "I don't know. I just don't know..."

Dr. Young watched me quietly for a few moments while I cried.

Then, as if reading my mind, she said, "Many things determine the course of a life, Connie. You cannot hold yourself responsible for everything that happened to Bonnie's."

I sobbed, "But if she had had her mother...it m-may not...have been so h-hard for her..."

She answered, softly, "Yes, her mother's death was life altering. But it is not necessarily to blame for every struggle in her life. The crash was not your fault, and it did not cause a chain of unfortunate events in Bonnie's life. Her life choices were and are her own. The bad things are *not your fault.*"

She repeated her last words a few more times as I cried, my head in my hands.

I knew that what Dr. Young said was true, but it was going to take time to accept. For most of my life, I had believed that I, alone, was responsible for every bad thing that life had dealt to either Tim or Bonnie. The belief was false, but it was still a belief that I needed to reprocess and eventually change. I knew I could not change it overnight, but that day, in Dr. Young's words, I felt a glimmer of hope that I could change it at all.

She was silent for a few more moments as I wiped the tears from my face with my palms and pressed my fingertips on my temples. I took a tissue from the box on the table next to me and dabbed at my eyes. Then I looked up at her.

"What can I do to help her?" I asked, my expression pleading.

"You already have," she said, "by caring."

"But it's not enough. I want to do more. I want to fix things for her," I said. "I'd sell everything I have if the money would take away her pain."

Dr. Young sighed. "Oh, Connie. You can't let this consume you. We all have to take charge of our own healing. We have to fix *ourselves*. And Bonnie will, with the help you've given her by showing up at all and by telling her how you feel. Just keep in touch with her. Let her know you care and are there for support, or anything else she needs that you can give her."

It was too difficult to explain why I wanted to do more for Bonnie than just be there if she called. In my mind, however subconscious (and erroneous) it was at the time, I had taken away her mother. Bonnie had traveled a painful road in growing into a woman without her mother, and without close relationships with other older women to comfort her during her formative years. On some level, I think I wanted to be that older woman friend to her. I was an unlikely candidate, but I wanted to be her confidante, her mentor, her secret-keeper—the one she never had. I wanted to be the one she came to when she had a problem, the one who protected her from further pain. I wanted to do for her and be to her what her own mother could not.

At the same time, I wanted a life. I wanted *my* life, not Pat's. I wanted to know what it was like on the other side, away from the storms in my head and heart and near the light of self-love and acceptance. I wanted to be with people and enjoy myself without having to fake it or fear emotional collapse. I wanted allow myself a future filled with happiness.

I tried to explain it all to Dr. Young, but what came out was more mixed up than what was inside. Soon, the hour was finished, and I left the warmth of her office for the cold of my isolation and confusion.

*   *   *

A few weeks after meeting Bonnie, my grandfather died.

Walter Grile, my mother's father, was ninety-three years old and had been in perfect health all of his life. He and my grandmother had moved in with us a few years after my father died, when I was in high school. He filled a room with his affable presence and keen sense of humor. A builder by trade, there was nothing he couldn't create or fix. Our farm bore his signature in the various cabinets, desks and other wooden works of art he made for my siblings and me and he knew everything there was to know about plumbing and electricity. He came to every one of my basketball games in my last two years of high school, cheering me on wholeheartedly.

When my mother made the move from country to city life, my then-widowed grandfather went with her. They lived together in a house built at the same time as mine and just a few blocks away. Grandpa oversaw the construction on both homes at ninety years old just to make sure the builder did things the right way. For twenty-six years—longer than my parents lived together—my mother and her father coexisted happily as best friends.

He was always there, like a father to me. It didn't matter that he never knew how the accident had affected me; it was enough that he was there.

And then he wasn't. Two weeks before Thanksgiving 2003, an ambulance rushed him to the hospital with what paramedics thought to be a hernia—the first major health problem of his life. He underwent surgery followed by complications. For eight painful days he was on a ventilator, and, as a family, we had to choose whether to keep him on one for the rest of his life or let him breathe on his own until his last. We chose the latter.

He died that day.

That was a month after I had met Tim and Bonnie.

*   *   *

It was at that point that I felt the vessel of my emotions splinter and start to take in more water than I could bail.

I mean, really! How much can one person take all at once? How much?! The question went through my mind often during that time, and it wasn't accompanied by self-pity. I was utterly confounded. The anguish that came with meeting Tim and Bonnie and hearing how their father had told them their mother was dead; the PTSD; the grief at losing a dear grandparent—those things didn't come with handling instructions.

I couldn't even separate which feelings applied to which issue, more or less figure out which issue to deal with first. There was no way I was going to figure out *how* to deal with the mess of them.

Then there was my mother, who had never been alone in her life. She had lost her father, whom she'd lived with for a quarter of a century—not counting the years she lived with him as a child and young woman before leaving home. They had eaten out for breakfast most every morning for years, something Grandpa loved to do. She had watched his favorite game show with him in the evenings for just as long. Her best friend was dead, and she faced an empty house for the first time in her life. I knew how hard this had to be and I knew she needed me.

I had nothing to give her, but I tried. I took her to breakfast the day after the funeral, after all the family had left for home, and we sat together numbly, two zombies staring at each other over our coffee cup rims. We ate takeout Thanksgiving dinner together at my house and spent the weekend after the holiday just occupying the same space. I was present only physically, and I'm sure it was the same for her.

*   *   *

By the following Monday, I was shrieking inside. I teetered on the edge of a total breakdown and I didn't want that to happen in front of my mother, who was in a bad enough place, herself, and who had no knowledge of what was happening in my personal life.

I can't take it anymore!, I thought. *I have to get out of here.*

And once I thought the thought, it became a mission.

I had to leave town, and quickly. Fortunately, I had scheduled vacation days with no plans.

"Where are you going?" Mom asked when I told her I was leaving, her voice thick with concern.

I could not explain to her that I certainly didn't *want* to leave her at such a horrible time, and that I felt torn because I knew we needed each other. And I did not want to tell her that I had no clue where I would go. I knew she would worry, and try to talk me out of it.

So I lied.

"I'm going to visit a friend," I said. "I planned it before Grandpa died."

It was utterly untrue, and I hated lying to my mother. But it sounded better than, "Mom, I'm losing my thin grip on my sanity and if I don't leave immediately for any destination at all, I don't know what will become of my life."

I had no destination. I had no idea when I would come back. When day broke, I just put a bag in my car, got behind the steering wheel, and turned on the car.

Then I drove away.

Chapter 19

When I got to the end of my street, I turned right and then left and then right again to get to the main road.

When I got to the main road, I turned right for no reason. Then I thought, *The best way to get to anywhere far away is the highway*, so I drove to the highway entrance. How far I wanted to go, I wasn't yet sure. I just knew the highway would take me there.

I was in no state to be driving a car. Flayed by my erratic emotions and attempts to hide my condition from those around me, I had begun crying the second I turned the ignition key. It had been more like an explosion, actually, when I closed my door—an emotional grenade detonating inside a sealed container. Sobs wracked my chest; I did not recognize the gnarled sound coming from within me.

What am I doing?! I thought wildly. *Where am I going? Oh dear God, please help me!*

My brain was incredulous at my body's actions, but my foot remained firm on the gas pedal.

I accelerated onto the interstate with the car's headlights slicing through the remnant darkness and stayed in the slow lane of the nearly vacant road. The few cars that passed me on the other side of the median drove briskly, their drivers with destinations, perhaps drinking cups of steaming coffee to keep them awake on the last leg of a long night's journey, perhaps taking in the morning's breaking news on public radio to feel a bit of human company.

I did neither. I just drove south.

For the first hour, I fought mightily against the urge to turn around. It took all my will not to veer across two lanes of traffic and yank the steering wheel hard left at a split in the median.

yearned to go back, but not just to my house. I wanted to be small again, a child with no concerns and nothing to do each day but play and explore the world. I wanted to wipe an eraser across the blackboard of my life and start writing from scratch in jaunty, backward letters with tiny fingers.

But as much as I pined for it, there was no going back.

The miles passed and I got further from home. The urge to turn back waned. My tears, and the rain that splattered on my windshield as I drove, did not.

Fat, lazy drops fell from the sky as if the clouds were buckling under their own sadness and letting it spill to earth. I drove on that way for some time, a strange cadence between the rain and the tears dropping onto my lap: *SPLAT-SPLAT-SPLAT, drrrrr-ip. SPLAT-SPLAT-SPLAT, drrrrr-ip.*

I glided between listening to its lulling sound and thinking of all that had happened to put me on the road to an unknown destination.

When I was sixteen, and sitting behind the wheel of a different car on a different drive, listening to music while the sun shone brightly, I never could have imagined what awaited in my life. If I had known, I would have pulled to the side of the road and waited long enough to let Pat's car pass before I continued the drive to school, or turned around and drove home. Our cars would not have collided, Pat would have lived, I would have been happy.

Maybe.

I was logical enough to know that God might have called Pat home then regardless of whether the accident occurred; that trauma and PTSD might have been in my future as the result of a different heartache. But for me, logic had always been the timid child and blame had been the bully.

Who can know what will happen in the next day or hour or second to drastically change the course of a life? Why, as humans, do we bow under a yoke of guilt for not knowing—and doing something to change—that which we can never know?

As I drove into the second hour of the trip, I knew that I needed to figure out where I was going, because I was not going home. It had to be a quiet place, where I could be with myself and be myself, somewhere no one would know me and I could unload my façade at the front door.

I scavenged the back seat floor with one arm while I drove and fished out a map of the country, then folded it into a manageable size and wiped my eyes to read the tiny print. Never veering from my southerly course, I had passed from Ohio into Kentucky at some point and left flat land for rolling green hills.

I looked for wide open space in the five-inch state picture on the map, outside and between the red lines of the interstates; places where a little green patch might mean trees and squiggly blue spots might indicate rivers or lakes. A place deep in the woods where people stood still to listen to nature was where I wanted to be.

And then I saw it: Daniel Boone National Forest.

I dropped the map on the passenger seat and composed a speaking voice, then punched the number for information into my cell phone. It took just minutes to find what I was looking for and make a reservation at a lodge in the heart of the forest, and I found that I was only an hour away.

Through fresh tears, I headed toward my destination.

*   *   *

Relief washed over me when, four hours after leaving home, my drive ended and I got out from behind the steering wheel.

As I closed the car door and looked up through the falling rain at the lodge sitting atop a winding, wet path, I felt calmed by the sight of the few cars parked in the visitor spaces—I knew my face had swelled horribly and I wanted to see a few people as possible in passing. There was no one outside, and the steady rain muffled any sounds that may have come from the surrounding forest.

For a brief moment, standing there in the silence, I felt as if I had pulled off daring escape from my life.

*   *   *

I dragged my bag and myself into the lodge to check into my room. The lobby was as quiet as the outside, and I was grateful. It had a woodsy smell and was lined with comfortable, squishy couches for weary travelers to fall into and rest while awaiting their turn for room keys.

The woman at the desk looked at me kindly, acting as if she saw guests with scratchy red eyes and raw noses every day. She smiled, and I forced one in return.

"How long will you be staying with us?" she asked gently.

I had no answer to the simple question.

"Can I let you know as I go?" I asked, instead, my voice nasally.

"Of course," she replied. "As you can see, we're not real busy at the moment."

"Thanks," I said, taking the key she offered and setting off to find my room.

The rear of the lobby spilled into a cavernous room that formed the middle of the lodge's first floor. As I walked into it, I saw the forest outside through ceiling-to-floor windows and smelled the smoky aroma of a fire crackling in a wood-and-stone fireplace. With a breathtaking view of the wooded mountains and ten times the same lobby couches, I knew I would spend much time there during my stay. I made a mental note of where I thought I might like to sit, and went to unpack my bag.

*   *   *

I did not leave the lodge for over two days.

I didn't watch television or talk on the phone. I did not read a newspaper.

Except for the woman who had checked me in and the waitstaff who brought my meals in the lodge's restaurant, I spoke to no one.

I was completely, voluntarily, alone.

For so long, I had never wanted to be alone. I hated being with just myself in my empty house—going out with people and drinking had been my method of dealing with my pain for nearly two and a half years. It had not made a difference that being with people—all of whom had been friends—and drinking until I was numb had never made me feel better. Although my disorder made me feel like a social misfit, I just kept doing it.

After all that had happened of late, my discomfort in social settings increased to the point where I could no longer fake normalcy in front of my friends and family.

Perhaps it was because I was so exhausted with trying to hide everything from nearly every one of those people—except for Mary Ann and Patty and Dr. Young—and so confused about trying to figure out whether or how to tell any of them. My disorder and my concealment of it had gone on for so long that it had grown into a monster; one that began driving me away from civilization and socialization the minute Tim had walked into my home. By the time my grandfather died, I did not even want to see another human being, much less interact with one.

And that's when I knew I needed to go away—not because I wanted to, but because I *had* to. I needed to be away from my job, and meeting friends for drinks after work, and taking business trips and attending social events and whatever else I had found in the last few years to fill my alone time.

As a social animal, I knew it wouldn't be easy to do. I had never been inclined toward periods of self-imposed isolation to reflect on my life; being alone with only my thoughts would be one of my greatest challenges. My safety net of human contact would be gone; I would be forced to walk the narrow high wire that was my mental state without it.

For two days, I sat in the great, cavernous room and looked out the windows at the rain-soaked forest during most of my waking time. I drank coffee and listened to the sounds of raindrops beating the rooftop and the flames licking wood logs in the fireplace. As thoughts formed, I scrawled them across sheets of new paper in my journal. I did my crying at night, in the privacy of my room, when I put my head on the pillow after a long, draining day of trying to make sense of it all.

Sitting in quiet solitude for hours made me start to realize that I *can't* make sense of it all.

I had been asking myself questions about the accident and its results for years, asking the "why" questions and the "what if" questions repeatedly until they made me see spots. They had plagued me for most of my life, and I had let them—even though I knew all along that they had no answers.

I wrote down the same questions in my journal at the lodge and as I later read over my notes, a thought formed: I could ask the same questions of myself and pose them in journals for the rest of my life, but they would shackle me.

Why was it *my* car that slid on that *particular* patch of black ice on *that* day at *that* very second, to force my car into Pat's path? Why was the ice there and not two miles down the road? I don't know. Why didn't one person ever want to talk about it with me? I don't know. What if things had been different? I'll never know.

They were questions that would bind me to the past. I would waste away, a prisoner waiting for a release that was not to come from the outside.

It dawned on me, there in the middle of the forest: the release needed to come from within me.

But how? I asked myself. *How do I let go of something that has defined my life?*

The moment in which the crash occurred had charted the course for the rest of my life to date. In my own mind, though not consciously thought, I had always been Connie Who Was in the Accident; Connie Whose Car Had Slid on Black Ice and Killed Pat Sloan. I was not a person separate from the accident; we were intertwined and always would be—me, the crash, and the other people whose lives had been touched by it.

Letting it go would be like severing an arm. As I wondered how I would even begin to do that, another thought came, and it was powerful.

I'm not the accident.

Wait, what?

It came again.

I'm not the accident.

What does that mean?

For hours, I picked it apart—turned it inside-out and around and upside-down. I saw a hazy picture in my mind of a younger me, before the crash. I was smiling and meaning it. There was no demolished car in the background, no cemetery headstone. It was just me.

I am not the accident?

It seemed as if it the thought made my heart a bit lighter. But, just as quickly as it had come, a vexing question followed.

What else am *I, if not that?*

*   *   *

I spent the latter half of my second full day inside the lodge asking myself that question and searching for an answer, or at least parts of one.

Nothing came to me. I had forgotten the person I was before the accident. She was a ghost, and the person I might have been if the accident had never occurred was a dream.

I had no clue who I was or how to find out.

Strangely, though, that fact did not concern me.

It was enough for me that, somehow, sitting with myself in reflection had led me to begin realizing that I was more than my past. A peace came over me and my tears nearly stopped. Oddly, so did the rain. For the first time in a very long time, I felt able.

I figured that the question of who I was would take considerable time to answer but the thought that, eventually there *might be* an answer, buoyed me.

*   *   *

On the third day of my trip, after a long, meaningful walk on the wet forest paths, I decided it was time to go home. I packed my bag and my journal reluctantly, not wanting to leave the still beauty and quiet of the lodge when, just a few days before, I had forced myself to come.

I left with a quieter mind and a calmer heart. I figured the rest would work itself out.

Chapter 20

When I returned from Kentucky, the holiday season was in full swing, and I found myself looking around and absorbing the scenery. By day, Christmas and Hanukkah decorations adorned store windows and every third car I passed on the road carried a fir tree tied to its top. Holiday songs played softly in the background as I did business at the bank, the grocery store, the dry cleaner. Saturday traffic swelled as happy shoppers scrambled to check gift purchases off their lists before time ran out.

In the evenings when the sun set early, the outlines of houses and trees and storefronts burst through the darkness in light strings of red, green, white and blue. Through living room windows, I saw families in my neighborhood trimming trees, their television screens glowing with scenes from *Miracle on 34th Street* or some other annual holiday special while they worked.

I thought of Pat in the picture Bonnie had shown me, standing on a ladder hanging her own holiday decoration. She had not known that her death was imminent; she was just living.

All around me, people were living life. Living was what I wanted to do.

I knew I had a lot of work ahead of me in figuring out how to do that, so I started small. I visited with my mother, and gradually began to see the rest of my family and some friends. I quietly immersed myself in the bustling holiday shopping crowds a few times and purchased some small gifts. I drank punch at my office holiday party.

One afternoon as I browsed through a local bookstore, just days after returning home, I happened upon the book *The Secret of the Shadow* by Debbie Ford. The title caught my eye and I began to read it in the bookstore aisle. I was soon thoroughly engrossed in the author's theory of the reason for the stories of our lives.

The following is from the first few pages I read that afternoon:

> Our stories have a purpose. Even though they set our limitations, they
> also help us define who we are so we don't feel completely lost in the
> world. Living inside them is like being inside a clear capsule. The thin
> transparent walls act like a shell that traps us inside. Even though we
> have the ability to gaze outside and view the world around us, we stay
> safely trapped inside, comfortable with the familiar terrain, bound by
> an inner knowing that no matter what we do, think, or say, we can go
> no further. Our stories separate us and draw clear boundaries between
> ourselves, others, and the world. They limit our capabilities and shut
> down our possibilities. Our stories keep us apart even while we are beg-
> ging to belong and fit in. They drain our vital energy, leaving us feeling
> tired, depleted, and hopeless. The predictability of our stories feeds our
> resignation and guarantees our fate. When we are living inside our sto-
> ries, we engage in repetitive habits, abusive behaviors, and abrasive
> internal dialogues.

I could scarcely believe the words—it was as if the author was speaking directly
to me! She confirmed what I had come to realize during my trip—that the crash
and Pat's death was the story I had been living inside for most of my life. I had
allowed it to define me as a person who took another's life, albeit unintention-
ally, and I had always unconsciously put that definition of myself first, ahead of
even my physical description.

Thinking back, I remembered times when this belief manifested itself—like the
times I had revealed the secret of the fatal crash to my few close friends and
significant others. I had been so frightened to speak the words, convinced they
would think less of me when they knew, as if the accident was all there was to
me as a person. In fact, none of them reacted in the horrific ways I had imagined. I wish that, like them, I could have seen the accident as merely part of the
story of me, and not allowed it to be the definitive authority on my identity.

I read on:

> Like all good stories, our personal dramas always have a theme, which
> repeats itself over and over throughout our lives. We can decipher our
> unique themes by listening carefully to the conclusions we have made
> about the events in our lives. These conclusions shape our existence and
> drive our personalities. Our conclusions become our shadow beliefs, the

unconscious beliefs that control our thoughts, words, and behaviors. Our shadow beliefs establish our limits. They tell us how much love, happiness and success we are not worthy of. They shape our thought processes and define our personal expression and squelch our dreams. But what's important to realize is that our shadow beliefs contain the very wisdom we need to transcend our current limitations and our discontent. They motivate us to compassion for our shortcomings and drive us to become the opposite of what we tell ourselves we are. Our shadow beliefs drive us to prove that we are worthy, that we are lovable, and that we are important. But, left unattended, these shadow beliefs turn on us, sabotaging the very things we most desire by letting their negative messages limit our lives.

Figuring out the theme of my own personal dramas was easy—I had allowed the shame and guilt of Pat's death to mold my belief that I was unworthy of lasting happiness. I had no feelings of self-worth and believed that I, a bad person, was deserving of whatever suffering the world chose to impart. My story had told me that I had stolen a person's life and a family's happiness, and that I must sacrifice my own to repay the debt.

Those negative messages had been limiting my life for too long. Why had I let them?

Ms. Ford says this in answer:

Our fear of change, our fear of stepping into new realities, is so deep that we desperately cling to the world we know. We often mistake familiarity for safety. The perceived comfort we derive from what is familiar keeps us living in the illusion of our stories. But the question we should ponder is, Are we really safe inside our stories? Instead of risking change, we hold on for dear life and resist the uncertainty of the unknown.

It was true: I had always found a distorted sense of comfort in feeling bad about Pat's death. I had opened my internal parlor doors to regret, remorse and sorrow years before and invited them to prop their feet and stay as long as they wished. Suffering had made me feel as if I was giving something back to her and her family; it was a memorial to Pat, and a penance for my sin.

Feeling awful had made me feel better, and it had been too terrifying to think of life without that pain. How could I go on living and be happy when she was dead? What would God think? What would I think of myself?

My mind had tired of resisting "the uncertainty of the unknown" for too long by the time I went to the lodge. It was there that, spent, it gave up the fight. I had left there knowing that I no longer wanted to live in the cage my story had built: I wanted a new identity and sense of self. I wanted to be more than the young girl behind the wheel of that car and the woman with post-traumatic stress disorder.

I wanted to feel found and whole, not lost and damaged.

The last line I read in Ms. Ford's book before buying it that afternoon was:

> In order to transcend our suffering, we must go against our instinct to hold on and instead surrender to the path of letting go.

Leaving the bookstore, I went a step further than I had at the lodge and gave myself a holiday gift.

I said goodbye to it all and took my first real, solid stride toward healing.

*   *   *

A week before Christmas, a greeting card arrived in my mail, addressed to me in handwriting I didn't recognize. As I opened it, a picture fell to the floor. I read the message quickly, and saw that it was from Bonnie. Then I read it again, tears welling in my eyes as I listened to her voice in my mind wishing me all the wonders of the season. I bent to pick up the picture from the floor, and turned it over in my hand to look at it. My tears fell on it as I stooped.

It was a picture of Alesha.

Letter to the Reader

The road leading to the writing of this letter to you, a fellow trauma survivor and PTSD sufferer, has been paved over the course of my whole life. Like you, I did not expect to travel this path, and there were many times I truly believed it led to nowhere but the destruction of my spirit. I wondered if I would ever look out across the horizon and see a new day dawn since darkness had always been my traveling companion.

My message to you is that there is light ahead for you. It is different than my light and that of every other PTSD sufferer, but it is there. Someone out there will care about you if you let them. They will listen as you talk, maybe even hold you while you cry, but you must first give your permission.

You must first *give yourself* permission to be cared for and loved.

For reasons unknown to my logical mind, I stopped giving myself permission to be happy, and cared for, and loved when Pat Sloan died. Of course, to some extent, it is natural to feel this way when one has been involved in a traumatic accident that has claimed another person's life. These feelings remind us that we are compassionate, good human beings who care for others and the sanctity of their God-given lives.

And grieve, we must. We grieve for what could have been, for the person who died that awful day, and for the person we were before the split second our lives changed forever. Grief is a normal reaction to trauma and death, an emotional processing that must take place fully and without regard to deadlines and timetables in order for us to live on wholly and healthfully.

But then—and when "then" comes is surely different for each of us—we must allow guilt and grief to take their graceful bows and exit the stage of our lives. They are only the first step in the healing process; we must leave them aside to make room for the next so that we can truly heal, and live again.

For over twenty years, guilt, shame and grief over Pat's death consumed me. Perhaps like you, I was young when it happened and I didn't know how to deal

149

with the emotional and psychological aspects of being involved in another's death. Although my family was very loving, and I had then and still have a very close bond with my mother and my siblings, giving me the emotional help I so desperately needed was too complex a task for them. They did what they could with the tools they had at their disposal, and I love them for who they are and what they were capable of giving me at the time.

My trauma happened when our country's interest in psychological wellness seemed, sadly, nonexistent—a time when American military soldiers were coming home from the Vietnam War with severe cases of a condition that would not be officially named "post-traumatic stress disorder" for another three years. Then, mental health was dealt with behind closed medical and personal doors— and that's *if* the traumatized person's caregivers knew enough to get them through those doors in the first place.

I wrote this book to tell you that your recovery need not take the same path as mine. Though I believe there is still somewhat of a societal stigma about the subject of mental health, there is help out there and it's on nearly every corner, even if it's difficult for you to see right now (please see the resources I've noted for you at Appendix "A").

It might be hard to find help now if you feel something is wrong but you're just not sure what it is (as I was for so long). I wrote this in the hope that you might recognize some of your own symptoms in my story and, with your new knowledge, reach out to a learned professional or PTSD organization to begin your healing journey.

The last and most important reason I spent the last year researching this disorder and making certain that I told my story in the truest way possible, was so that you, a survivor of a fatal car accident, would feel a kinship in your suffering. Since my diagnosis, I have scoured the Internet, bookstores and libraries to find everything I could about PTSD, and there was nothing specific for us, the community of those who survived a car crash when someone else died.

I wanted to share my story so that you know you are not alone. I have been where you are, and I'm here for you.

You may have seen your own story unfold as you read mine. If that is true, then my wish for you is that you garner the strength to share it, face it, and move beyond it to live the rich, full life you so deserve.

Wishing you all of God's blessings,

Connie Bachman

onnie Bachman

Please visit my website at

www.conniejobachman.com.

I would love to hear your story and welcome your comments.

Special Thanks

Thank you Tim and Bonnie for meeting with me and allowing me to share with you what I had wanted to share for so many years. This came at a pivotal point in my healing process and I thank you for this wonderful gift. Thank you also for supporting me to share my story with the hope of helping others.

References

Ford, Debbie. 2003. *The Secret of the Shadow: The Power of Owning Your Whole Story.* New York: HarperSanFrancisco.

Matsakis, Aphrodite. 1996. *I Can't Get Over It: A Handbook for Trauma Survivors.* Oakland, CA: New Harbinger Publications, Inc.

Matsakis, Aphrodite. 1998. *Trust After Trauma: A Guide to Relationships for Survivors and Those Who Love Them.* Oakland, CA: New Harbinger Publications, Inc.

Matsakis, Aphrodite. 1999. *Survivor Guilt: a self-help guide.* Oakland, CA: New Harbinger Publications, Inc.

Panos, Angie. 2002. "Healing from Shame Associated with Traumatic Events." In *Traumatic Stress and PTSD Articles.* Retrieved May 31, 2005 from Gift From Within web site: http://www.giftfromwithin.org/pdf/healing.pdf.

Rosenbloom, Dena and Mary Beth Williams. 1999. *Life After Trauma: A Workbook for Healing.* New York: The Guilford Press.

Williams, Mary Beth and Soili Poijula. 2002. *The PTSD Workbook: Simple, Effective Techniques for Overcoming Traumatic Stress Symptoms.* Oakland, CA: New Harbinger Publications, Inc.

Appendix A

American Psychological Association
www.apa.org
750 First Street, NE
Washington, DC 20002-4242
(800) 374-2721 or (202) 336-5500

Center for Journal Therapy
www.journaltherapy.com
Promotes the power of writing and how life-based writing is one of the most reliable and effective ways to heal, change and grow.

Center for Stress and Anxiety Disorders
www.albany.edu/csad
For those who live in the Greater Capital Region of New York State (for purposes of participation in stress and anxiety related studies and treatment assessments)

EMDR International Association
www.emdria.org
Informative website pertaining to Eye Movement Desensitization and Reprocessing (EMDR).

Gift from Within
www.giftfromwithin.org
16 Cobb Hill Rd.
Camden, Maine 04843
(207) 236-8858
email: joyce3955@aol.com
Joyce Boaz, Executive Director

Matsaksis, Aphrodite, Ph. D.
www.matsakis.com
Licensed Counseling Psychologist
Specializing in PTSD

National Center for PTSD
www.ncptsd.org
Has a vast "Highly Selective" PTSD resource section

National Institute of Mental Health
www.nimn.nih.gov
National Institute of Mental Health (NIMH)
Public Information and Communications Branch
6001 Executive Boulevard, Room 8184, MSC 9663
Bethesda, MD 20892-9663
(301) 443-4513 (local) or toll free (866) 615-6464

PTSD Alliance
www.ptsdalliance.org

978-0-595-38974-2
0-595-38974-0

Made in the USA
Coppell, TX
08 September 2022